RUDGWICK
MEMORIES

Peggy Walker

ᘧΕ

D. J. ELLIS

Fernwood, Nightingales, West Chiltington,
PULBOROUGH, West Sussex. RH20 2QT

Designed and
Typeset in 11 on 13pt Baskerville

by   David J. Ellis

Fernwood, Nightingales, West Chiltington,
PULBOROUGH, West Sussex. RH20 2QT

Printed and Bound in Great Britain by
Billing & Sons Limited
Worcester

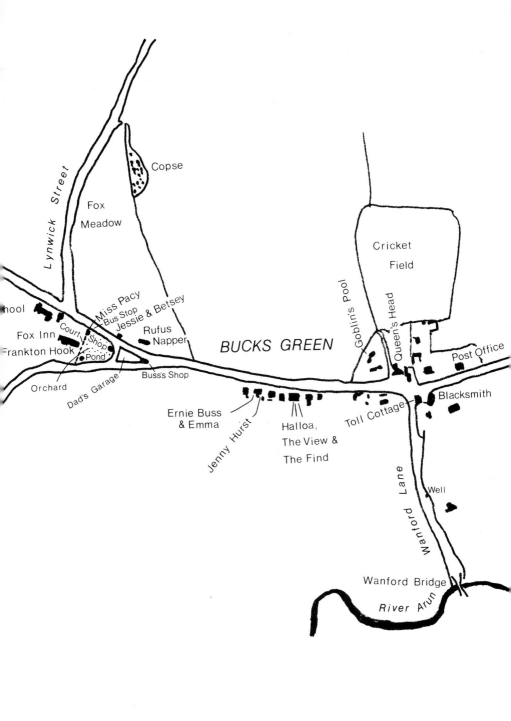

ACKNOWLEDGEMENTS

Wendy, for her kindness in typing my work.

The Misses Boxall, for the loan of photographs.

*My daughter, Carol, and son, Bernard,
for their constant encouragement, without which
this book might not have been written.*

*I dedicate this book
to my grandchildren,
Caroline and Jessica,
and all Rudgwick children.*

CONTENTS

ILLUSTRATIONS

Rudgwick Memories

Main Road, Rudgwick (Rudgwick Street)

I awoke to the sound of rain falling on the
ivy leaves that climbed up the old elm trees. It
was not quite light. I lay there, going over again
the dream I had had last night. As I am getting
older I seem to dream or remember my happy childhood more and
more often. People say you can remember only the happy times:
if so, how wonderful; I wish this on all children in the world.

*Frankton
Hook*

Once more I was back in my large room. It had to be large—
or I thought it was—for I shared it with my two sisters, Barbara
and Molly. Our house was called Frankton Hook; it was the end
part of the Fox Inn, in the village of Rudgwick. This is the house
where I was born. Rudgwick is a small village divided into four,
very spread out: Rudgwick, Bucks Green, The Haven and Tismans
Common. As a child I remember it as one—we didn't seem divided;
we were 'the people of Rudgwick'. We had four public houses, or
'Ale Houses', as they were called, because they sold only ale. The
men didn't have to go far for a drink, and women just didn't visit
pubs with their menfolk. I remember my father would be in 'The
Fox' twice a day, and if we needed him we would just 'rap the
wall'. I never remember my mother going in there, ever.

The Fox Inn from the front

The Fox Inn is quite old, 16th century. At one time it was a workhouse or where men could get a night's lodging. They would come from Brighton to Rudgwick and then on to Guildford. I can remember that my father used to dig up little silver-coloured discs in the garden — these were what the men used to hand in for a night's lodging. The men would also have to make themselves useful by sweeping up the yard outside and maybe chopping wood, etc.

One day an old man came, so dirty it looked as if he hadn't washed for a year. The keeper's wife said, "We can't let him get into our beds like that. You must give him a bath." Two of the other inmates offered to help. The old copper was fired in the copper-house, the tin bath brought out filled with piping hot water. What a treat! They washed the old man and let him soak awhile, but when he stepped out of the bath his body still looked black. They decided amongst themselves to throw the water away and try again with fresh water, as the first lot was rather thick. This was done and — as they rubbed and soaped the old body for the second time around — they found he had a vest on . . .

The main part of 'The Fox' was where the inmates were. (When repairs were carried out, they found some little cell-like rooms down in the cellars on the left.) Where I was born was where the master and people in charge used to live.

The outside was covered with that lovely crimson red Virginia Creeper, so every time I awaken to the sound of rain falling on the leaves I think of my happy home as a child where I was born.

The Bottings — Barbara, Humphry, Michael, Molly, Peggy and Val

The house was quite large—room for us six children, mother and father. We were three boys and three girls. I always think large families are happy—there is always someone to do things with.

There was a large court outside, with a stone sink and an iron pump. That is where we got our water from —straight from the well. We took turns to fill the two buckets that stood in the kitchen; we had a sink there but no tap. The court was made of red bricks. I well remember how slippery they got when wet. There was an open drain, and the water ran down, then it went underground to the ditch outside our garden. There was always a smell there on hot days. Our toilet was a brick-built 'little house'. That was what it was always called—no indoor sanitation; to put it crudely, 'bucket and chuck it'. It had a fence up the side, and no one seemed to close the door when using it. Often as children we used to rush up, to hear a loud clearing of the throat with a grunt from my Dad sitting reading the newspaper. On dark days he would have a candle with him. The 'little house' was built beside an elderberry tree. The roof, covered with ivy, seemed to be my brother Val's favourite place in hide-and-seek. Once we found one of our hens had a nest up there with eggs: thought she was safe from us children, I guess. There were two seats in the 'little house', one large, one small. We knew no other way, so it didn't bother us —but people who came from the large town thought it was dreadful. It all went back on the land: I can see my Dad now, digging the large trench.

We had a large garden with a pond for my Dad's beloved ducks. Under the quince tree just one side of the French window, Dad made a table with a bench either side. All summer we children had all our meals there. Somehow the summer was always warm. We had all the fruit trees and Dad grew what we needed in the way of vegetables.

Many Pets Mother's great joy was her rabbits. Our local butcher was also keen and Mother and he used to borrow each other's bucks. One day I heard him say (or thought I did), "Put the buck and doe together on a nice Sunday morning." Up I chirped, "Why Sunday morning, Mr. Butcher?" "Not Sunday, silly; I said *'sunny'*." was the reply.

Dad kept pigeons and if Mother needed something for dinner Dad would go into the run, pick them off one by one, and wring their necks. I well remember the odd pheasant hanging up in the dark passage-way. Why the dark secret? I used to think; they all belong to God. You see, we kept chickens, ducks and had many wild rabbits. In those days most men would put down a trap to help feed the family. I still think of those lovely rabbit pies and stews. Women had time to cook in those days. As you see, there was not much money but we lived well. One day Mother had some baby ducks under a wire frame on the lawn. Mick, Val, Barbara and I were catching them and putting the frame back when we accidentally dropped the frame on one of the ducks' heads, knocking its eye out. There it was, hanging. Mother was out and we couldn't kill the duck, so we got a bucket of water and drowned it. To this day I can hear his little feet going 'flip, flip' on the side. To say the least, Mother was cross—"Duck could well have lived with one eye. Just pick it off: ducks cost money," she said. Dad just said, "Well, in all my life I have never heard of anyone drowning a duck!"

The house was large and roomy, with three bedrooms; one for the girls, one for the boys and Mother's and Dad's. There was always a baby in there, or so it seemed. Then the attic; just a little room, under the sloping roof. It used to fascinate my sister and me. We would grope around in there, among the boxes with all kinds of treasures; old clothes, broken furniture, pictures. Everything seemed just to have been thrown in out of the way. There was a little window covered with dust and cobwebs. Mother used to say, "Don't play in there, Peggy; you will come through the floor." It frightened me, but all children like to be scared if they have someone with whom to share the adventure. We all thought there were witches up there, as we could hear the birds under the eaves fluttering. In the Autumn, Dad would clear a space and store the apples on newspaper on the floor. In the night we would hear the rats—they would carry the apples to the head of the stairs and let them roll, Bump! Bump! Bump! down. In the morning there would be three or four apples on the stone floor in the kitchen. We were really scared; I hated the rats and mice in the skirting-boards, squealing in the night. If I could smuggle the cat up to bed with me, I would. But then what happened was, when Mother came to kiss us goodnight, which she did every night, she'd say, "Have you got that cat, Peggy?" The purring sound made the bed tremble and, as Mother whipped back the bedclothes, took the cat to the window, leant out and dropped it, I squealed. "He will land on his feet," said Mother. He always did.

We forever had cats around. Mother would only give milk to the cats if they had kittens. One day up in the shed at the top of the garden we watched a cat give birth to four kittens in the old tea chest. There we were, leaning over the top, watching every detail. I always think country children need no sex talks as it's all around them with the animals.

We children used to argue amongst ourselves when we were in bed. My Dad used to bellow along the passage, "I want to hear no more; you can get up at six o'clock tomorrow morning and fight it out on the lawn." I never remember doing that, so I suppose we all shut up. I can never call to mind ever being hit by Mother or Dad. One way Mother would punish us, and how I hated those dreaded words, was to say, "Peggy, you will not go out of the garden for a week." She meant just that: it was to school and straight back. My best friend would stand at the back steps and ask if I was coming out, but that was more than I dare do and we were not allowed friends in. The circus came to the village; my elder sister came home to take Val, Michael and me. Mother said, "You may take the boys, but Peggy is in the garden for a week." Even though it was the last evening, Mother would never go back on her word. A week was a week and it made no difference that the circus came only once a year.

We had many pets, even a pig at the bottom of the garden. Most cottages did, as people tried to be self-sufficient. One day, coming back from a day out down the river, we saw these black stubble hairs with traces of blood in the outside drain. They had killed the pig on the court outside. The neighbour would have come in to help, for 'a bit of bacon'; then we would have helped him with his pig. I can only remember this happening once, so I expect it was stopped later on.

We had three cows at one time — Milkmaid, Buttercup and Daisy. They belonged to us three girls, and Mother would take them up Lynwick Street. At the Fox end there were wide verges where we would have to stay with them to watch while they ate the lush grass. The cows were tethered down and we would help Mum milk. Have you ever tasted milk straight from the cow, warm and sweet?

Also, we had a white rabbit, which was 'our pet'. How many times did Mother call up the stairs, "Have you fed the rabbit, girls?" when we were in bed? Only to hear we had forgotten again, so Mother would nip out to feed it. Dad said, "If you don't feed that rabbit it will die." One morning we went down, to find it dead in the cage. We rushed to Dad, but all he said was, "I told you it would die if you didn't feed it." Dad had broken its neck. You do not forget again, given a second chance.

At our home there was a court, six bricks wide, laid end to end from top to bottom of the garden. As children we all had to weed this, cutting out the weeds in between with old knives. It was about 100 yards long, but seemed forever to us. I hated this job as the boys used to put the worms down our necks.

Dad was very fond of ducks. He had Khaki-Campbells, which were kept overnight in coops at the top of the garden. Just over the hedge was a bus stop and every morning Dad would let *Ex-Guardsman Drills Khaki-Campbells in Rudgwick* the ducks out and they would waddle off down the court, Dad ordering them "Left, right, left, right . . . " Half-way down, there was a gap in the hedge. Dad would shout, "Left wheel!" and the ducks would peel off to the left. The people at the bus stop looked in amazement. "Look at that!" they would exclaim. What they did not know was that there was a pond on the other side of the hedge and the ducks would have gone that way anyway! What could we say? "Ex-guardsman drills Khaki-Campbells in Rudgwick!"

I never remember Dad killing any of the ducks to eat, but we had many eggs, which we often had to look for if the ducks laid out. The ducks would eat the wild garlic around the pond and I thought that made the eggs taste 'oniony', so I didn't care for them.

One day Dad was resting on the sofa. I rushed in. "Dad! Dad! The ducks have gone down the Fox!" Dad opened one eye. "Don't worry," he said, "they won't serve them!"

You must never let ducks out too early or they will lay in the pond. I helped Dad clean out the pond once. There were a number of eggs on the bottom in the mud, so we had lost them. Like my Dad, I just love ducks.

I remember especially the baking days we used to have. We had a large brick oven. I can see now the large kitchen with its stone floor. The oven was fired *Baking Day* with faggots, bundles of brushwood placed right into the oven. The heat would come from the ashes when it died down. Then the ashes were raked out. I can see now Mother making the loaves of bread—standing the dough in front of the oven on a table to warm and rise before putting it in with the long wooden peel.

With our large orchard, we had trays of apples, and apple pies. Mother used to make enormous slabs of gingerbread, currant buns, slabs of cake—things like that. It used to be so wonderful on baking day. We girls would always love to help in the warm, cosy kitchen. Whose turn would it be to lick out the bowl? Mother taught us all to cook very young. You never forgot.

Here's a little story I must tell you about baking day. We always kept ducks and chickens, as I told you. I remember an occasion when the old hen had forsaken the six duck eggs she was sitting on. They were nearly hatched, so Mother thought that after she'd been baking she would put them in the warm oven overnight. This she did. When she came into the kitchen the next morning, she could hear, "Cheep! Cheep! Cheep!" Mother lifted down the heavy iron door — and there were six little ducks, running round and round the oven because the bricks were hot to their feet.

Sometimes Mother would take almost-hatched-out eggs to bed with her under the quilt.

Bucks Green Post Office (now an antique shop)

At the top of the court near the main road, at our end of the Fox Inn, was a little one-roomed cottage. A Miss Pacy lived there, a little bird-like woman who wore long dark clothes. She always had a black apron on, and a little bonnet when she wasn't wearing a white lace cap indoors. She *Miss Pacy* was an old lady when we were children. I can remember her taking her 'slops' down to our 'little house' each day; she carried them under her black apron.

I loved to go up to her door with a bunch of wild flowers, for on some days she would ask me to come in for a chat and sit by her black grate with the bright fire. I remember her room, full of 'everything', the pictures on the wall, the mantle shelf with the velvet green runner with bubbles on the ends, her large clock which she would never put on or back— she didn't believe in it. She had red-patterned seats to her chairs. Sometimes she would tell stories about when she went to "The Dame School", her mother paying 3d a week so that she could read and write—which not many children

Twice one are two,
Baby's little shoe.
Twice two are four,
Lying by the door.
Twice three are six,
Let us pick up sticks.
Twice four are eight
Put them by the gate.
Twice five are ten
To roast the big fat hen.
Twice ten are twenty,
Now we have plenty.

had the chance of doing. Lesson books were few and expensive, so children were taught in rhyme. Sometimes she would tell me some and I loved to hear them; even though she was an old lady she seemed to remember them well, so it couldn't have been such a bad way to teach, even if it was parrot-like repetition.

When the girls left school they were expected to complete their school life by

Thou shalt serve no God but me,
Nor unto Idols bend the knee.
Take not the name of God in vain
Nor dare the Sabbath to profane.
Give to thy parents honour due,
And never shalt thou murder do.
In every word and deed be clean,
Steal not, for thou of God art seen.
Speak thou the truth and always love it,
Thy neighbour's goods thou shalt not covet.

producing beautifully-worked samplers. Boys of eight or nine would often work during the spring and summer months scaring the birds, and tending pigs and cows, for about 6d a day. Miss Pacy said we were lucky, as we always seemed to be at play. There was a large red curtain at one end of her room and we could just see the bed peeping out. We were not invited to look behind the curtain, but would dearly have loved to. Miss Pacy seemed to do all of Mother's mending. In return, Mother would send her up the delights of 'Mother's Baking Day', while we older children would carry up her buckets of fresh spring water from the old pump, run her errands, mostly for reels of cotton up at Miss Dinnage's, or nip down to the Post Office at Bucks Green. We kept her little cottage filled with fresh flowers and she would read to us from her large black bible. She taught us many things and we gave each other a lot. She was sadly missed when she died.

King & Barnes, who owned the Fox, pulled down the cottage to put in a car park for the Fox—they knew the 'Motor Age' was to come. We children had just started to sit on the old shed and take the numbers of the cars that passed by. At that time the road to Guildford had deep ditches on either side, with flowers growing on the banks. We would climb down the ditch to pick wild violets, white and mauve. Only the white ones would smell sweetly, but both were so pretty.

I remember the day my father set a rat trap in the ditch. Later in the day he caught a rat by the leg. I cried and cried because he wouldn't let it go as it was still alive. I was always soft-hearted; I couldn't bear to see anything hurt and would even pick up the flowers that had been dropped and put them in the water in the ditch.

*Swimming
in the
River*

Dad had a lot of time for us children. He would take us along the river bank observing natural wild life — water-voles, kingfishers, snakes, beautiful dragonflies and, of course, birds' nests, including swans, sometimes, with nests with young. I used to think my Dad knew everything about the river. He taught us all to fish, but I didn't like it—I couldn't bear to put the worm on the hook. Of course, Dad was born at "Wanford House", right on the river, so I understood his great love for it. We had wonderful days at the river. I can feel now the stubble of the wheat scratching my ankles as we made our way across the fields to our beloved river. Our part there was a high bank where we would leave our food and clothes. I remember I had a bright yellow costume. It was the only costume I remember having as a child. Maybe it was the only one! Later on I remember swimming in my vest and pants, when we were older and had moved to deeper parts of the river.

We would clamber down the bank, which was thick yellow mud. To the left, the water was shallow and crystal-clear, as it slipped over the stones. There were mussels that we could collect and prize open, only to find a jelly-like mass inside—what we did with them I do not remember. We would make dams of the mud and I can see now the yellow streaks mixing with the clear water. Dragonflies would dip over the water with their glossy blue and green wings glistening in the sunlight. Water voles would nip in and out of the banks, and the old water rat would show himself. One day we actually saw an otter. I expect he was tempted by the many small fish that darted over the flat stones, for otters come out mainly at night. They will fish and play with their cubs on the banks of the river on bright moonlit nights, a very pretty sight which I saw once at dusk when I was walking home with my Dad from the old mill where he was working. One would see the otter's tracks in the mud all along the banks of the river. Oh, the happy days we spent down at the river!

To the right was what we called the deep part. There was a willow tree bending right over the water. Just beyond this was a deep hole. It seemed miles long, but really it was only about 115 yards. We would walk into the hole, tread water (like riding a bike) on our toes as high as we could, straining ourselves so that we could catch hold of the willow, leave go, and then we were on the other side. That is where we all learnt to swim, each egging the other on. I guess we all just had to swim. I found it so easy, with no fear of the water, and I never seemed to feel the cold. I could swim along the river when I was only four, with the others cheering me on running along the bank. I just took to the water like a duck and I have always enjoyed swimming more than anything. They could never get me out of the water. Mother had a brass gong which she hung on the apple tree, and she would sound it when she wanted us all home. Being a large family, we always had someone to do things with.

When we were all better swimmers, we went down to the floodgates to swim. It was about ten feet deep on the mill side. I well remember a retired bank manager who would be there. Before entering the water he always plugged his ears with long bits of cotton wool. The younger boys watched this with great interest, for all self-respecting country children believed in ghosts in those days, and the boys always felt there was magic somewhere in this cotton wool disappearing down his ears, to be followed by diving into the river. This was almost a ritual affair. On a warm summer evening quite a few would meet.

There was a tunnel which fed into the dip pool and we would slide down the tunnel into the dip pool. The fishermen there used to shout at us, as we disturbed the fish. But we did have fun. We would swim right up to the hunting bridge and back, with all the flowers — kingcups, irises and meadow-sweet — growing on the banks, the cows in the meadows watching. No one minded; we did no harm and I don't remember anyone drowning, as we all looked after each other, especially the younger ones. Once I dropped my younger brother, Michael, into the little brook that ran down to the river. I can see him now, lying on the bottom, his little white hat floating off and away. Barbara, two years older than me, grabbed him up and he didn't seem to have come to much harm.

We had great fun in that brook, paddling, making houses on the bank, putting pieces of wood up for shelves, finding old bits of china to put flowers in, laying dry ferns on the floor. We used to make our own fun. One thing we always played was 'boat races'. We would make our boat out of anything. We made a great thing of Oxford and Cambridge Boat Race Day: we would buy these celluloid dolls with feathers and skirts of light or dark blue. I was Cambridge. We would go around chanting, "Cambridge the winner, Oxford the sinner, put them in the matchbox and throw them in the river." There was great rivalry among us children at school.

One day I was in our bedroom changing and eating a 'Black Jack' (a kind of toffee bar made of liquorice), when I dropped it. I looked everywhere, under all the beds. The other children were yelling, "Come on, Peggy! We are going; come on!" I was desperate; I dropped onto my knees and felt something hard—there it was, stuck to the underside of the coconut mat. I grabbed it, dropped on my knees again and said, "Thank you, God". I really believed in God. I never could sing and I always envied the Tate family at school, as they all had beautiful voices (at one time there were nine of them in the village choir). One day at Sunday School I was told about some people in a barn. They were passing around the harp and at each turn they sang. One man couldn't sing, so he prayed, "Please God, give me a lovely voice"—and when his turn came he sang 'like a lark'. For years and years I sent up that prayer; but no, I still can't sing.

Another game we would play was tracking. Two would go off, and leave chalk arrow marks on flat stones and trees. The rest would follow after about fifteen minutes. We would run for hours till we would find them laying in an old barn in the hay. We would all rest awhile and then someone would say, "Let's look for birds' eggs on the way home." First we would look for the barn owl's eggs, then make our way to the pond outside to find the moorhen's eggs on a little island in the middle. (So it meant an excuse for a paddle.) Most country children had a collection of birds' eggs in a box with sawdust. We would only take what we needed and we always left at least two in the nest so the hen would lay again (and she usually did). We all knew where each kind would lay, robins low down, rooks high in the trees. Then there were the lovely little wrens' nests — how wonderful, how clever — all woven with feather and wool that the sheep left on the barbed wire we crawled under. The nests would withstand the wind and rain.

No country child would ever pull out a nest. If we met a gamekeeper, which we did sometimes, he would be cross and say, "Birds' nesting, which way did you come in?" We *The Gamekeeper* would point and he would say, "Go back the way you came"—but we would always be sure we pointed the way we wanted to go. One day to our delight we saw a hedgehog going round and round. He had been sucking a pheasant's egg and had got half of the shell over his eyes. It was lucky for him that we had found him before the gamekeeper—we let him free to see again.

Sometimes we would come across a piece of wire strung high between two poles. Tied onto it were dead and dangling weasels, stoats, squirrels, rats, magpies, crows, jays, sparrowhawks and other predators. The gamekeeper would have to rear pheasant chicks by placing about twenty eggs under broody hens, which he would keep in coops in a clearing in the wood. The sparrowhawk was very smart at nipping in between the coops, as the very young ones ventured out away from mother's care. The gamekeeper had a hard time, as until the young would roost in the trees, they could never be left night or day. At night they would 'jug' in the long grass, so they had to be taught. This was done with the help of gun dogs, which would never hurt the chicks. The keeper would beat the ground and the dogs would rush around them until they flew into the trees. It didn't take long to teach them and in time they would go up at dusk, often sticking to the same trees every night. To feed the chicks, the gamekeeper would catch and boil rabbits. They would have to be well-cooked, as all the meat had to be put through a very fine sieve so that no small bones could be in the feed. (Just like a baby, I thought.) I used to feel sorry for the pheasants. They were almost hand-reared and, as you can imagine, were so tame that in the autumn when they used the beaters to raise them so that they could shoot them, they almost gave themselves up. I never did think there was much 'sport' (as it was called). Men and boys could get a day's beating for two shillings (men) or sixpence (boys), plus bread and cheese with ale, so I suppose it was good in that way.

When we children did come across the 'gamekeeper's pantry', as that array of rotting dead animals and birds was called, we were fascinated and frightened to see the bleached skulls, the claws and the sharp teeth, close at hand. I never knew if this 'vermin pole' was to scare the other animals and birds, showing what could happen to them, or to impress the boss, who would often walk along 'the rides' with his guests on shooting parties. One thing one would never see strung up was a fox. Even if the boss didn't hunt, his guests might. The gamekeeper would trap and shoot foxes, often using a dead cat for bait. (When they came near the pheasant chicks, cats were shot, buried and dug up later for fox bait.) It was best on a rainy day, as the fox would run down the ride looking for an easy dinner. The keeper would place the cat in a little gully place and set about seven traps around. The fox was bound to run into one and was caught and shot while running off with the cat. One gamekeeper said to his boss once, "Shall I shoot the odd fox?" The reply—"Do as you wish, but do not tell me." Foxes do a great deal of killing for killing's sake. Have you ever seen a chicken run after a visit from 'Freddy Fox'? Chickens lying around with their heads bitten off.

Gamekeepers were often asked to help with other wildlife problems. One old man, sitting by his cottage door, told the keeper passing by that he was losing all the goldfish from his garden pond one by one. Both agreed that it must be 'Jack Heron', and the keeper came the next day as the dawn was breaking, gun under his arm, and saw a large black cat sitting at the edge of the pond. Smartly dipping its paw in and scooping up a large fish, the cat ran straight by the keeper with the fish in its mouth. The keeper didn't like to shoot the cat, as he thought it might belong to the cottage.

On our way home from the woods we would often stop at the little brick bridge and have races with little sticks and see whose would come through first to the other side. Who could make that flat stone skim over the water how many jumps? We would arrive home hungry and tired, but happy, with bunches of wild flowers for Mother, who was always pleased to see them around the house in the jam and paste jars (and there were elderly ladies who always welcomed flowers).

Every Sunday we would go to Sunday School at the little St. John's Mission Church at Tismans Common at 3 p.m. They still have the same pictures on the wall; the chairs with the straw seats, wooden floor and the hassocks to kneel on; the small altar with the snowy white lace cloths which Mrs. Skinner washed for free for over fifty years, and the golden cross on the little stone font near the door. In the dark winter for evening service a gang of us children from Bucks Green would go to the big church on the hill at Rudgwick for a kind of adventure. There was a big sanatorium for T.B. up the street and we children would hold our breath as we got to

Sunday School

it and then run like mad till we were past it. (In those days the cure for T.B. was fresh air, so in the daytime you would see the patients sitting out in the grounds, winter and summer, or in bed with every window and door open. One bitterly cold day a stranger passing by asked a local who were the people living there? His reply was, "Idiots!") At the service, my thighs were so cold that my girl friend would rub them as we sat at the back of the church. One evening we were just going down Gaskyns Hill, on the way home, when we saw this large white thing, with what looked like long white arms to catch us by the hair. We were very frightened and decided to make a dash for it. The faster we ran, the nearer it seemed to be coming. I remember dragging the little ones along, and at the bottom of the hill we discovered that it was only the white signpost at Watts Corner . . .

Rudgwick Station

The 'plum' for going to Sunday School was the Sunday School outing — one day a year, to the sea by train. I can never remember the station-master being cross with all us children swarming all over the platform, as you bet we were there a good hour before the train was due! The excitement, the joy: how we looked forward to it for weeks ahead. Packing our little cardboard cases—bottle of ice cream soda for me, piece of Mother's apple pie,

and cake. Not much money, maybe, and
of course that yellow swimming costume.
Mother used to say that she could spot me
right down at the water's edge. Would it

*Our One Day
By the Sea*

be a fine day? The day before, we watched to see if the cat was
sleeping on his head, which was a sign of rain. Also we would
dash into the garden to see if the little red pimpernel flowers were
open or closed. If they were closed it meant rain. You know, I
don't recall a wet day. We took paper streamers to hang out of the
train windows. On the way back we blew through the tin whistles
which we bought at the sea for three pennies. Once let loose on
the sandy beach, we liked the tide out best. The little rock pools,
crabs that walked sideways, shrimps that were not pink as we knew
and had for tea sometimes. Jelly-fish and finding and keeping that
prized piece of seaweed, which hung on the gutter over the back
door for almost a year to come. Mother would stick a long pole in
the sand with a flag on top, so that we could find her. We ran back
like homing pigeons. Mother would keep her eye on children whose
mums couldn't come. Those lovely castles with the moat running
around them, pretty stones all pressed into the sand, the buckets of
water for the moat back and fro, as it dried up so quickly. All day
we would play, until those dreaded words, "Time to meet up with
the others, get dressed". I never had any dry knickers or socks to
go home in. We just needed that last paddle, then that big wave
came too high for me and my sandcastle. Mother said it would.
Tired, but very happy, we dragged up to the station, buying Dad a
piece of rock on the way. He loved peppermint. He never seemed
to come with us on these outings. I guess someone had to mind
the animals. That night we'd say our prayers in bed: "Thank you
God for a lovely day. I will keep going to Sunday School."

We had in Rudgwick what we called the 'big
houses'. There lived the people who made the
work. At Pallinghurst there was an enormous
estate. The old farm cottages down Barnsfold

*The Big
Houses*

Lane, Tismans Common, were the homes for the farm-workers. I
can see now the yellow-and-blue-painted farm-wagons, and hear
the clopping of hooves and the jingling of the harness as they went

tramping along the muddy by-ways. No one seemed in a hurry in those days. The workmen worked long hours in the summer. Winter was hard. If it rained, they donned sacks split up one side to form a hood and cloak combined. If it was frosty, they blew upon their hands and thumped their arms across their chests to warm them.

Most boys leaving school were taken on at the farm as a matter of course if their fathers were farm-workers. Labour was cheap and the land was well tilled.

Another house was Gaskyn's, right in Rudgwick Street. Mr. Barker there thought himself the 'lord of the manor'. I say this in a nice way, for he gave a lot of work to the village. He owned a lot of land, right out to Dedisham. The number of house staff was high, as with eight children they were needed. At one time there were eight gardeners.

On large estates married staff outside the house were given cottages. Single gardeners lived in a 'bothy', a house or large hut in the grounds, where they all 'mucked in' together. So you may guess what a mess they were in, living and cooking there!

The house staff worked long and hard hours. Rice pudding and soup were made there and given to the poor of the village. Mr. Barker gave the organ to Rudgwick Church. He was a strong churchman and in the church choir.

In the shooting season the family would go to Scotland for six weeks. One year, the resident cook didn't want to go to Scotland. Working as a kitchen-maid was a little village girl called Mary. The lady of the house called Mary and said that when they went to Scotland she wanted her to take over the cooking. Mary said yes. "If you buy me a cookery-book, Madam," she said, "I will do my best." Which she did, never having less than eighteen guests in the house.

When they came back to Rudgwick the lady called Mary into the dining-room. She said: "Thank you very much, Mary. You did well in Scotland. We are very pleased with you. So I'll give you tomorrow off." This shows you how out of touch they were with the working people. What an extra shilling would have meant to Mary! The lady hadn't had to pay her regular cook during that time. No, she thought a day off would be enough.

A bit of old Sussex.

Martens Cottage and Stubbons, Lynwick Street

Another large estate was Lynwick House. A German lived there. He cared much for the village and how it looked, and took such a pride in it that he would employ two men on a Saturday to walk around the village. You would see them with spades over their shoulders. Their job was to dig in any litter left lying about. The German would ride a large black horse. The tale goes that one day the horse was stung by a wasp and threw him, and from that day on he would give 2d to anyone who brought him a Queen wasp. So the children had a field day. Also, he kept his ditches in such good order that on their way to school down Lynwick Street the children would make little boats of matchboxes and sail them down in races. He came before the 1914-18 War and was more or less kept a prisoner there for the whole of the War. At the top of Rudgwick there was a forge. The shed is still there, opposite Hawkridge. The German actually employed a forge-worker, as he wanted all his land surrounded by iron fences. If you go along the Red Footpath that runs along the old railway line, you will still see traces of this fencing, with the old 'kissing gates', as we called them. There is one just by the old bridge in Rudgwick Street and another at the back of the Queen's Head.

The village cricket field, football ground and tennis courts were all enclosed with these fences. When I was a child there was always some sport, e.g. stool-ball or rounders, for us to play there in the summer evenings.

The man from the house was a kindly man. I expect he was lonely. He used to go down to the rookery in the woods to feed his rooks. We always called that wood 'the bluebell wood', as there was always a carpet of blue under the rookeries in the spring —helped by the droppings, I guess!

When the German left Lynwick House, a new family took over. I will call them 'the Lewises', although this was not their real name. Mr. Lewise treated his staff very badly; they were overworked and underpaid. Local girls would not work for him in the house, so he would get girls down from the North and pay them about £1 per month.

His wife was an old dragon. Those girls worked long hours and had little time off—and what chance was there of getting their fare back North? Once two ran away. Late in the evening they got to Baynard's Station. They told the station-master that they had fallen out and Mrs. Lewise had kicked them out, not letting them take their 'boxes' with them. The station-master rang up our local policeman, who came up on his bicycle, heard the tale and found one of the cottages nearby to sleep the girls overnight, while he went to the big house and told them that he wanted those two 'boxes' at the station in time for the eight o'clock train to Guildford in the morning. He also wanted the money owing them for their fare. If they did not agree, he would get the case sent to Guildford, where the Lewises knew a lot more would come out once it was in the local paper. So they begrudgingly gave in.

There was a gamekeeper working for another large house nearby. He was once having a drink of ale in the Queen's Head when he met up with Mr. Lewise's gamekeeper, Mr. Bond. The first gamekeeper told Mr. Bond that a fox had got into his aviary and killed his whole stock. [All gamekeepers would have their own aviaries near their cottages with, say, fifty hens and five cocks. They had to put pheasants' eggs under the broody hens when rearing the baby pheasant chicks. These aviaries were completely covered in with small-mesh wire netting on all sides and over the top.] Well, Freddy Fox had found a little hole to put his nose in— and country folk say that if a fox can get his nose in, he is in! And not only can he get in, but he'll get out the same way! And this is what this fox had done. He had killed the lot. Heads were bitten off, wings and legs torn apart, and maybe just one eaten.

Mr. Bond said: "I can let you have some eggs. I have more than I need this year." This was arranged and done. The game-keeper who had lost his stock told his boss, who said: "How very kind. I will write and thank Mr. Lewise."

When the letter was received, Mr. Bond was sent for and sacked on the spot. He had overlooked to tell his boss of the eggs he had given away. Mr. Bond had to get out of his tied cottage, with a family of six, and he could never get another job as a game-keeper. Everyone knew what had happened, and in the big houses people would hang together. So he took a job on the roads.

I always remember the daughter of the house riding her horse. She had a very, very large bust, which would bob up and down in her tight jumper. No bra — or 'brassiere', as they were called in those days! Small boys would open gates for folks on horseback, hoping for an odd copper. If it was only "Thank you, sonny", the boy would say in a soft whisper: "Yeh, I got a pocketful of them"!

One of the reasons Lynwick House became empty again:— The master had a farm-worker in a cottage who came up to the front door one morning early with his gun, asking to see the boss. When Mr. Lewise came, the farm-worker lifted the gun to his own head and blew his brains out. There was a great fuss made. No one seemed to know what had been said between them before it happened. And most was hushed up. The people in the village said the farm-worker made one mistake—he should have blown Mr. Lewise's head off, not his own!

No one was sorry to see that family leave. But one thing I must say. The public driveway through the grounds (about two miles of it) was most beautifully kept in the spring-time: masses of daffodils, snowdrops, wild violets, primroses, lining the driveway. A joy to all who used it, thanks to the hard work of the gardeners.

Bottings' Rudgwick Stores (opened June 1908, closed May 1917)

When my Mum and Dad were first married, they had a shop opposite the Martlet Hotel on the corner, where they sold flour, corn, seeds, home-made bread and cakes, sweets. The only trouble was that the Martlet opened at 8.30 and Dad did spend rather a lot of time in there. At last the shop closed and they moved down next to the Fox, where for me it all began.

Dad went to the War to do his bit, like so many of the young men of the village, for four long years.

*   *   *   *   *

Dad Coming Home From The War

One of the first things I can remember is my father coming home from the First World War. Barbara ran to meet this tall man in a soldier's uniform, who picked her up as he was walking along by our orchard hedge, coming from Rudgwick Station. I ran indoors crying to Mother: "An old man has taken Barbara away!" I was about three years old: maybe I was seeing my father for the first time, as he was away in France for the duration of most of the War.

When Dad came home there was no work for the men. What had they been told? "A land fit for heroes!" "A piece of land of your own to farm!"? That was if you had worked on the land before. (Also, if you had, you were the first ones to be sent home at the end of the War.)

You were told: "Every man must do his duty!" — with Kitchener's finger pointing at you. Oh, well, promises are cheap; not so, lives. What hardship if your man hadn't come back! Dad got an old wooden shed put up in the corner of our garden, facing the road. At first it was used to store grain. We used to play in the bins. Dad sold wheat, corn and bran.

Wanford Mill

Most cottages kept a pig, chicken or livestock of some sort. Dad worked the Wanford Mill for a while. How we older children used to love to go down and watch! The corn coming down the chutes, the bags of flour dragged *Wanford* up by the chains through the trap-doors to the *Mill* top, the great leather belts turning the wheels. "Keep clear!" Dad would warn. He had good reason. His younger brother, Sam, was killed at eighteen in the Aldershot Mill: his arm was caught in the open belts and he was crushed to death. It is all written on the tombstone in Rudgwick churchyard. We children would solemnly read it out to our friends, basking in the limelight for a while because we knew all the details first-hand—with a little added, I am sure.

Then there were the large stone mill-wheels. Dad would chip out the grooves. We sat around watching while Dad told us tales of what it was like when he was a boy.

He was born at Wanford House. They said there was a tunnel under the mill-pond in front of the mill. It came up in the house. Dad said he used it, but wouldn't ever let us children. Too dangerous! The water had seeped in, bricks had fallen in. Dad wouldn't even show us—in case we tried, I suspect.

But what was a delight to us was the huge water-wheel on the side. When it was not turning we would clamber up to the top. There was just a wooden privy seat there. It would have been much easier to use the bushes—but no! Up we went, one at a time. It was quite a feat, climbing that great wheel, and there was the deep water below. I never remember a slip from any of us. I thought we were very brave. My heart would thump away; I had to follow the rest. Whether we really wanted to use it or not was not important. It had a fixed bucket under the seat, which was flushed out as the great wheel turned. Of course this was not the same as our little house at home. Emptying of this was a daily chore for Dad (for Mother while the War was on).

Dad was a keen fisherman. The mill-pond was a favourite place for pike, or 'jacks', as Dad called them. He found a rotten dead rat by the side of the pool once and used it for bait. He caught a 12-lb. jack. That evening on the way home he offered it to the local fish-man, who had started a fish-and-chip shop. He sold the fish for £1:10s. It made really super thick steaks. All the customers wanted more the next night.

Mostly we ate the fish Dad caught. I can see now the headless eels (you had to cut the head off to get the hook out) in the stone kitchen sink. Mother was very fond of eels. The large jacks were hung on hooks in the copper house.

One day Dad put a large jack on a bender (which is a piece of hazel-tree) right through the fish's head. And we carried it home. He said that if it fell off, on no account were we to pick it up, because it had a lot of razor-like teeth.

Although we carried it up the road, Barbara and I, it dropped off just by the Queen's Head and we had to knock on the door and ask old Mr. Merritt—who lived in the old toll-house; you will notice the brick-work—if he would put it back on the bender. It was an enormous thing, you see. The great head with the needle teeth, although dead, would hurt you badly. We children always thought that maybe they weren't *quite* dead.

In the spring-time it was so pretty down and around the old mill, the banks of the river lined with wild flowers. I liked the golden king-cups that grew in the water, the water-lilies, meadow-sweet and wild iris; yellow and white mixing, with the primroses and small wild daffodils; and the pale purple milkmaids in the water-meadows.

One day Dad noticed two wild ducks on the river at the back, with nine little ducklings. Every morning he fed them with tit-bits. But one morning one duckling was missing; the next day, maybe two. Dad thought, "Rats. Must be rats. They are more than fond of ducklings."

When they were down to three left, Dad happened to be looking out the back door of the mill very early one morning, when he saw that enormous head with those killer teeth take two ducklings at once—in one gulp. But I'm sure Dad got his own back, for he loved to fish every day.

One day he caught a perch, which is a scavenger fish and will eat anything. He had caught it by the eye. He pulled it in and removed the eye with the hook. After throwing the perch back in the river, he thought he might as well use the eye for bait. He threw the line back in the water. And the first thing he caught was a one-eyed perch!

He also told a tale of catching a black cat. One day he pulled his line in and was throwing it behind with a small fish on the end, when he felt something tugging from behind. Puss had swallowed the fish and the hook! You can imagine the trouble Dad had killing the cat! (How else could he get the hook out?)

Now a much happier tale about our dog, Rex. One spring we children went for a Saturday walk along the river bank, when we noticed a large hollow tree-trunk on the bank. We decided to push it in, and as it hit the water with a large splash, out swam five little brown things which scrambled up the bank, into the field and away. Rex stood there, too frightened to move. We had disturbed the rabbits' warm, cosy home. But one day, on another river walk,

Rex did better, As we walked along, we saw a deer and fawn jump out just ahead of us. The fawn was so confused that it jumped into the river, which was not too deep at that part. But it just stood there. *We* didn't know what to do, when all of a sudden Rex lunged down the bank into the river and, holding the fawn by the scruff of the neck, pulled it to the side to safety.

Another part of Rudgwick was Tisman's Common. When you think of the name, 'Common', you would naturally assume that it should be just that—a common or piece of common land. Well, although we children used to play football there with proper posts, it all seems to have gone now. There are hedges all around now. At the top of the hill was the Cricketers Inn. Very recently some new people came to the pub and changed the name to 'The Mucky Duck'. No cricket was ever played there, they said! But that is totally wrong. Cricket was always played in the fields around it! And the lane that runs along the back is called Pigs Lane and pigs and cattle were taken along the lane to feed by the wayside when we were young.

And now a sad tale about the little brook at the bottom of Cricketers Hill. One morning a man's hat was noticed floating there. It belonged to an old man who had been missing for a day or so. Police dragged the river higher up, at last finding his body. He had fallen in while fishing.

Mother's Little Shop

When our family had grown to six, Mother thought it would be better to change from corn to selling sweets and tobacco and having a tea-room. We could make more money, and could always put little tables out in the orchard behind. Dad used to keep the lawn cut very well and it looked so pretty under the apple trees. This we did. And in the summer months later on when the few cars came on the road, I remember we children would sit on the shed roof in the evenings and take their numbers.

Mother sold almost anything: rabbits hanging up outside, 6d each; the jars of sweets; tins of toffee—'Super Palm', all flavours 3d a slab; fruit; eggs hanging up in a wire basket. We did quite well, really.

One traveller would fascinate me by taking three eggs, making a hole in the top and sucking them, one after the other. This was his dinner, he said. Mother had a large box which the men would sit on. She would serve them large white mugs of tea with her own home-made apple pies, gingerbread or meat pies, which she would buy in. The lorries were just beginning to come on the road then.

But before that there was the General Strike, 1926. I have never been able to forget it . . . the continual stream of men that were on the road where they'd come up from Wales to look for employment in the area. They were very shabbily dressed, with their shoes falling off their feet. And they always used to have a kind of large cocoa-tin, with a handle made out of a piece of wire. They'd have a little bit of tea in the bottom. They used to come into Mother's shop and ask, "Can you spare a drop of water?" Mother always did, and she would give them milk and sugar and something to eat. I have always considered that my mother was a good, kind person, because she never refused help to anybody; and yet she had six children to bring up with not much money.

Across the road from our shop were three very derelict cottages. In the first one, I remember, there was a brother and sister called Jessie and Betsey. And — the truth — you would sometimes look across from the other side of the road and see the odd rat walking along the window-sills! Once the old man was bitten on his forehead by a rat while he was lying in bed. Everything was so dirty. I remember the doctor used to come in and say to my mother, "Will you come in with me to see the old lady, Mrs. Botting?" She was ill in bed and Mother had sent for the doctor. She always went in, and when she came out her light-coloured stockings would be covered with fleas.

Mother was kind to the old couple. And we children needed no second telling to take in the odd cake or some soup. We would like the chance to look around, just like all children. There was just a path through the house, with the dirt piled up on either side of it. I can see now Jessie lying on those filthy rags called his bed. And there was Betsey trying to cook on an open fire, her rusty black alpaca dress sweeping the ground. And she always had a little bit of dirty white lace around her neck.

One day my mother, who always took care of her own appearance, could stand that lace no longer and quickly ripped it off. Betsey, who was almost blind, said, "What's that?" "Nothing," said Mother, "Just brushing something off your shoulder!"

Some time later the old lady fell down in the road outside the Bucks Green Post Office. The doctor came and decided that for their own sakes she and her brother should be taken into the work-house.

The cottage was burnt down—it was little more than a wooden shack—and literally you saw the rats and lice come across the road. The other cottages were infested, and so were the Fox Inn and our house. I well remember catching the fleas in bed with a piece of soap, and taking some wild yellow flowers to bed with us to stop them biting us, as we thought. At that time a garage was across the road. The owner used to sleep in there, but he couldn't stay because of the fleas. They just came across the road to keep him unwanted company.

Dad used to keep the orchard smooth and green. He had us children cutting out the weeds and sweeping it with a large broom made from a bundle of hazel-tree branches. We had to pick up any leaves left. Sometimes Dad would yell out: "Hey! Look what I've found!" And he would hold up a shining two-shilling piece which he had put there minutes before, making quite sure we didn't see it before he picked it up. The little ones would say, "Cor! Say we found it!"

We never hung around too long. It was never, "What can we do now?" Dad would always find us a job, even if it was only holding a piece of wood he was sawing. We would run errands. Maybe I would come home from school and Mother would be waiting: "Peggy, run up to Miss Dinnage for a reel of cotton!" This was next door to 'The Plough', half-way up Rudgwick Street. Miss Dinnage had a long counter, highly polished. She used to sell elastic by the yard. We used to ask for hat elastic. (We didn't like to ask for knicker elastic, which was what we really wanted.) There were laces, reels of silk and cotton and safety-pins. How I longed to handle the silk and laces. Miss Dinnage would wear a long black silk dress, trimmed with white lace, and a little white lace cap. I thought she was so rich and beautiful. She kept our village draper's shop.

There was a shop at the top of the hill, Mr. Humphrey's, a village store with a post office at the back. We didn't have many shops. Before these came, a lot of people who lived in the cottages would put home-made sweets in their windows because they wanted the extra money. They would make and sell almost anything. Mother used to make ice cream to sell, a great luxury. The ice-man would call. I can see now the large blocks of ice wrapped in sacking, sixpence a block. He would go to the fish shop in Horsham and call on his way back to Guildford. We used to lower the ice-blocks, tied in a sack, down the well to keep them cool until we were ready to use them. We had a sort of wooden bucket with a handle at the top which you turned. It took for ever. Mum would make the ice cream like custard. She put it in a container which had flappers, and packed this around with ice-cubes. The handles turned the flappers.

Mother would usually make this on Sunday afternoons and all would come for their 1/2d cornet. It was a sell-out from the start. Mother was very fair and would save us children some. We never had ice cream like that again. We had another container which needed no turning as it had no flappers. We just packed it around with ice. But the ice cream from that one only had an icy taste.

We children needed no asking twice to turn the handles of that first ice cream machine with the flappers—for weren't we allowed to have the flappers at the end to lick clean? I can see us now, sitting on the little brick wall on the back court.

Sometimes Mother would make ice cream in the summer evenings if the ice-man came by. Word soon got around the village: "Bottings' have ice cream!" And the children would rush up.

Val and Michael eating Mother's ice cream, sitting on ice-blocks (1928)

One summer, quite a few of the cottages each took one or two boys from Battersea for a two-week holiday. They had a good time! They used to walk around the village, singing:—

> "We are some of the Battersea boys!
> We all know our manners;
> We all spend our tanners.
> We are some of the boys!"

Battersea
Boys

I can picture them now, sitting along our brick wall at the front gate, smoking 'Woodbines'. We village children got on well with them. One day, as we were jumping over the brook from a high bank, Tommy (one of the boys) cut his knee badly. We took him home to Mother. She never panicked. We had an Aunt Jane who was a nurse in the War. We always sent up for her.

By the time she came, Mother had held the knee under the pump and let the water gush over it. It must have been painful. Aunt Jane sent one of us for the doctor, who laid Tommy on the kitchen table and stitched the knee skin back on. We all went to the top of the garden, but we could still hear the shrieks of agony; in those days he would have been given nothing to ease the pain.

But the boys enjoyed the countryside, running in the fields. Once, one of them gave a yell and came running back to us. "Hey! I have found a cow's nest!" he cried, and he showed us a pile of empty tins of milk.

Of course, they got up to some mischief, and one sneaking village lad was always telling the village policeman. But the boys got their own back. We had all gone up to the railway station to see them off. The village lad was standing by the bridge jeering at them. The boys from Battersea chased him down the Red Footpath and gave him a good hiding before they left. We all just watched and said: "Serves him right."

The
Carrier

We had a carrier in the village who would go to Horsham on Wednesdays and Saturdays with his horse and covered cart. He would call for orders in the mornings. He would get anything; he charged 3d an item and would bring the things back in the evening. Sometimes he would give one of us children a ride, delivering around the village. We were happy to do the running, just for the ride.

I also remember a tall man, a Mr. Hollingworth from Ewhurst, who came with large cases on the back of his bike. It would amaze me what they contained. The stuff just tumbled out: ladies' underwear (brightly coloured with lots of lace), dresses, shirts, men's ties, socks, etc. "ALL YOURS FOR 2/- PER WEEK!" was the slogan. Thus they tempted us to buy.

As children we only used to go to Horsham once a year. Mother paid so much a week into a *Market* shoe-club. We used to buy our shoes from Phelps in *Day* the Carfax. The great treat that day was that we went by train. Mother would make it a market day. The market was just outside Horsham station. We really loved that. There were all kinds of wonderful things for sale: colourful balloons, windmills on sticks that whirled around in the wind, a toy wooden monkey which—when you squeezed the two sticks together—would climb the ladder and swing over the top. There were many sorts of brightly-coloured clothes, toffee-apples, aniseed balls, sherbet fountains, plus all the live animals. I wanted to buy them all! I couldn't bear to think they might be killed. Sometimes Mother might buy a box of day-old chicks, which would be lovingly, carefully carried home on our laps in the train.

Mother always seemed to buy some 'treasure': an old piece of china or a chair, the odd fancy rabbit that took her eye. All were willingly carried home for her by us. What a day! All this and those bright new shining shoes that we promised ourselves we would never get dirty or wet and would polish every day. And if the money went that far, Mother would buy a pair of rubber boots for us to paddle through the floods at Wanford, along the brook in winter. (Somehow we always seemed to let the water come over the tops of the boots and we would have to hang them upside down in the high kitchen for days to dry out. Mother was always cross with us for this.)

Mrs. Secretan, who lived in the large house, 'Swaynes', on the Horsham Road, started Guides *Guides &* and Brownies in the village. My sister Barbara and *Brownies* I joined the Brownies. Mother made one firm rule —if we joined 'anything' in the village, we would have to stick at it, not leave in the first two or three months. "So give it a lot of thought," she would advise us, and we *knew* Mother meant what she said.

It was quite a long walk from our house. We would go on a Saturday morning. The first weeks we started, every Saturday was warm and sunny. How we longed for a wet morning, as Mother had bought us these lovely blue water-proof capes with hoods attached (we had so few new clothes—that is why I remember it so well) and she wouldn't let us wear them unless it rained!

Eileen Tuff and Barbara were Patrol Leaders. I wasn't over keen. I liked the tracking over the fields, church parades and working to get the badges. But my great love was swimming. We only had the river, which was frowned on by most (not clean—too dangerous—who would take us?). There were no swimming baths nearby, so what chance did the village children have to learn to swim? (We were lucky, as I have related — our family all went together, teaching each other. But many parents wouldn't let their children use the river, except for the odd paddle.) Eileen and Barbara went on to be Guides, but even their enthusiastic account of camp life did not impress me to join.

No! I was not a good Brownie, but I had to stay until I was too old to be one. However, I must say the people who run the youth organizations deserve much praise and support, for they do a wonderful job, giving up their spare time (no pay), their only reward knowing the children will grow up to be better citizens, wanting to help others, they hope.

The Chapel   And now a word about the people who ran the Chapel. They would give the children treats, super picnics in the new-mown fields up at Ellens Green.

They would take them in the farm-wagons and there would be races afterwards and little jars of strawberry jam as prizes. We would go to the meetings in the Chapel and the teacher would go around the class and we had to say a text out loud. I would always say: "God is Love". And there to this day it is written on the wall. I never did seem to remember to learn a new one.

Mrs. Lipton played the organ and kept time with her dentures. They used to click as she talked, and she had a habit of clicking them as she played. So we had, for example: "Onward, Christian soldiers! *Click-click!* Marching — *click!* as to war — *click-click!*"

We went to the Band of Hope in the Chapel and we all signed the pledge at about ten years of age. We thought it rather silly at the time — we were much too young. But we enjoyed the evening out and the treats.

We had some real characters in the village. One, a Mr. Charman, lived in Wanford Cottages over the river. He was a short, square, jolly man. He used to follow the hunt with his two small terriers. His job was to dig out the fox when it went to ground. I have always lived in fox-hunting country and always thought that bit was rather unfair. "Surely, if the fox got *that* far . . . ?" But then I thought about the chickens in the runs. They couldn't even get out! So I have come to the conclusion we mustn't take sides.

Village Characters

Anyway, when Mr. Charman got older, maybe too old to follow the hounds, once or twice a week he would put on his old, faded red jacket and his rusty-coloured black hunting-hat — obviously given to him years before. And from the old brick fireplace he would take down his long brass hunting-horn and then, with two little dogs at his heels, he would make his way up through the village. As he passed the cottages he'd sound the horn as he went along, and the dogs used to run and follow him.

At our gate on the Loxwood Road he would give an extra blast. Our old spaniel dog and terrier we had in those days would be sleeping under the chair as Dad was reading by the fire. Those dogs would be up, and they'd go rushing down the long court. And though my Dad would swear and call them back it was as if those dogs were struck deaf.

I can see the old boy now, in his faded red jacket. By this time he would have about twelve dogs at his heels, and be making his way up the hill on his way to Tisman's Common for a day's rabbiting. He would be gone all day, and then, just as it was getting dark, he would come back. We children, who would be sitting on the steps waiting, would see him coming down that hill where the butcher's shop is today, the dogs so tired at his heels. He would have the long bender over his shoulder with the rabbits threaded on by their feet. As the dogs came to our house, our own two would slip past our legs and up the court. They would be absolutely filthy, with lots of thick yellow mud underneath their stomachs where they'd been down those rabbit-holes most of the day. Old Mr. Charman would slip off a rabbit from his bender. "Here you are, Peggy! Give this to your mother!" he would call out, as he threw it up the steps to us children.

I used to wonder why Dad got so cross when the dogs went. For didn't we get the rabbit? Most welcome with six children always ready for a meal, I used to think. It wasn't until I was married and living in a little cottage with a dog of my own that I found out the answer . . . Some mornings I would see the little terrier from the cottage up the road sitting outside our gate. If our Lucy came out into the garden he would give a little "Yep!" Lucy's ears would prick up. She would make a dash through that gap in the hedge and away they would tear up the road. I would run to the gate and call in my stern voice, but no way would Lucy take any notice.

My husband, just like my father, would get cross over this, for they would be gone all day 'hunting'. But often dogs will get into mischief and worry sheep. In that case the dog-owner must pay the farmer for the damage and the farmer is also quite entitled to shoot the dog. So at last it dawned on me: Dad had thought that Mr. Charman would teach the dogs bad habits.

My Dad used to say it was no good beating the dog when it came home. It thought it was doing the right thing in coming back. The only thing to do was to try and get someone to give the dog a good thrashing when it was out. But as Lucy limped home covered with mud, you didn't know whether to kick her or kiss her. We were kind of thankful she had made it home safely.

There was another lovable old character, a lady. This was a little later, when my mother had her shop. You will notice that most of the things were kept outside on a wooden bench: fruits, sweets; well, almost anything. Now this lady had been a cook in service, so she had good money when she was younger, but now she was retired. She always looked so smart (some women always look nice). She would pick blackberries to sell, and mushrooms and flowers for extra money, for she too did like a drink at the

Fox. Every morning at lunch time (opening time), you would see
this stately lady with her bag walking up to our shop, but not
buying. What she was really doing was helping herself to the odd
orange, etc. This made my brother Val mad. "What annoys you,
they do not think you know." So one morning Val sat in the back
of the little green van, looking out of the back window. Up came
the old lady, and she had two oranges in her hand as Val burst out
of the back door of the van. "Ah!" shouts Val, "Got you this
time!" At that she flung the fruit at him, yelling, "Take your
bleeding oranges then if you don't want me to have them!" She
made Val feel quite guilty. The outcome of that—nothing—what
could you do? Just look the other way when she passed by our
little shop, for she was a War widow and had worked hard all her
life. Many of us owe a debt to others.

There was a young man who would catch moles. I remember
meeting him while I was walking over the fields at Pallinghurst
picking wild strawberries. He was in bad health, so he did this to
earn some money, getting 1/- for a pelt. He hated to see those
little brown soft furry animals with pointed noses dead, but he
needed the money, and the demand was there. Some 'ladies'
needed their fur coats in those days, it seems.

In another of the cottages lived Rufus Napper, a well-digger.
He was a bachelor, a large, striking man with a full head of red hair
and a beard. Water is quite easy to find in this area, but all well-
diggers hoped it would not be too near the surface, as they were
paid by the foot (1½d a foot). They often worked together. Hard
work sometimes! Once, the other two with Rufus said he was not
pulling his weight, so they nipped over to the Queen's Head for 'a
quick one', leaving him down the well, where he had to wait until
they came back to wind him up.

Rufus lived on his own. There was always plenty of work for
the well-digger, who worked with a water-diviner. My Dad could
do this. Also, I remember my Dad letting me have a go: as I held
the Y-shaped hazel stick by the two prongs, the other end would
turn up if there was water below where I was holding it. They said
it was a gift: not all could do it. I can remember when water was
laid on in Rudgwick just before the War: Dad went along to help
before they laid the pipes. But I have never used my 'gift'.

As children we were always seeing Rufus sleeping off his drink. I heard our Dad say he would dig a well and then get drunk. In those days you could do it for 1/6d (I think the beer must have been stronger then.) Once I saw him asleep in a ditch, head on one bank, feet on the other, with the water running over his tummy. And he had his hat on! Another day the boys came to school and said they had seen him asleep down the coalman's yard on the coal, covered in frost. One day at dusk he was quite merry from the pub and went into Billy Butcher's for a pig's head. Said Rufus, "Leave the eyes in, Billy! I want them to show the way home!"

There was an old lady in the village who had a donkey cart. She used it to collect firewood. She would scare us children, but I don't think it bothered the donkey. Then there was another lady who was a dress-maker and had an adopted daughter called Livingstone, who had been found abandoned on a grave. Nobody knew her name, so she was called 'Livingstone' because she had been found alive on a tombstone. And then there was a man in the village who used to trail his wife about in a Bath-chair attached to the back of his old high two-bar bike. We would see him on his way to the Fox Inn. We knew all these village characters. They were loved by all.

In Bucks Green there are three cottages in a row, built by a man who was very fond of fox-hunting. He named them 'Halloa', 'The View' and 'The Find'. In the first one lived 'Gig' Napper. He drove a little gig with a little high-stepping Welsh pony. A notice by his gate read: 'Water-Diviner and Well-Digger'.

A little higher up was another cottage and Jenny ('Aunt' Jenny) had a little hut in the garden with a bell outside. It was a big bell and you tugged on a piece of wire and it went clang-clang-clang-clang! The back door of the cottage would burst open at the sound of the bell. Out would bustle Jenny, wiping her hands on her black apron. She was a lovable, happy, round person. I remember we would buy aniseed balls (20 for 1d), gob-stoppers, locust beans (½d each) and nougat with cherries and nuts in. If we had money we would rush to buy these delights. Years later this sweet shop was burnt down and Jenny was able to build a room on the cottage for a shop. I expect she quite missed the trot across the yard!

Next door lived Mr. Buss with his daughter, Emma. Up near our shop was a small brick-built *Buss's* little hut. It was at one time used as a flour-house. *Shop* (The flour was used for giving to the poor—guess the poor had got richer!) Anyway, Mr. Buss used it for snodding — mending boots and shoes. The shop had a stable-door. How we children loved to hang over that stable-door and chat! Mr. Buss really loved children. He was a little old man, a cripple. He used to sit on a chair facing the window and he had a great leather apron on. He would lean his crutches in a corner. When he wanted to reach something, he would use one crutch and hop like a bird, much to our delight!

And I can see him now with large sheets of leather stacked up. He would take up the large curved knife he used to put the leather on the shoe, and cut the sole out. And it always used to fascinate me to see his well-used thumb with the very long nail kind of edging this round, heaps of little chips of leather lying on the floor. I remember the lovely smell of cobbler's wax, his old high-back wooden chair, the odd picture or two on the white-washed walls. In one picture, 'The Village Football Team', and in another, 'The Old Mill'.

There was a wooden bench just inside the door. All were welcome to sit and chat. Maybe there would be a man out of work, or a service-man home on leave; they would sit and talk to Mr. Buss, and I used to think how lovely it was that he'd got time to listen and people had got time to talk. Tales were told like the day Johnny Horner stood leaning on the half-door at Ernie Buss's shoe shop, when a man in a car (a rarity in those days) pulled up and called out: "Hey there! Can you tell me the way to Wisborough Green?" The old man looked a bit confused. "Well, now," he muttered. Then he took off his old felt hat, scratched his head, and said, "Well . . . Wisborough Green . . . well, you could go that way, or . . . then again . . . you could go . . . no, no—that ain't no good! Well, you'll better go . . . " The motorist started to get impatient. "Come on, man: how do I get to Wisborough Green from here?" Johnny Horner replied, "Well, mister, if I were going to Wisborough Green, I wouldn't start from here in the first place." And with that he put his hat firmly on his head, called good-night to Ernie Buss and strode off down the road. Meanwhile a verbal punch-up was developing in the shop as to the best way to get to Wisborough Green. Young Bobby Barnes thought you should go up Cooks Hill because there was a sign-post there (good thinking). Harold Boxall thought you should take the Tismans Common road; the man in the car was waiting, trying to get a word in . . . until Mr. Bacon, the school-master, came along and sorted it all out. How we lived in those days—real excitement!

As a child I would take Dad's boots down to be mended, and after school Mother might say, "Run down, Peggy, and get Dad's boots from Mr. Buss!" And I used to say, "How much are they, Mr. Buss?" He'd smile, then say, "Oh, bring me down an ounce of baccy and a box of matches!" Nut-brown tobacco was 10½d, matches ½d—coming precisely to 11d. But I think he was really being kind to my mother, because everyone liked my mother. I found after she'd died and I was grown up, people in the village would turn round and say, "Oh, I remember your mother. She always helped people." What a nice thing to say of someone!

Later on, the people in the village built a serviceman's club at Tisman's Common. A Mr. Verrall used to brag that he had bought the first share in this for 1/- in Buss's shop from my Dad, who was one of the people who started it.

I remember helping to unpack the yellow chairs when they built the club. They built it very much to the front, although they had land at the back, little realising that in the 1980s almost every working-class man would have a motor-car. They never thought in 1922 that they would ever need a car park.

Mr. Barker of Gaskyn's was very much against this club because they were having drinking there. But they got the land, a quarter of an acre, for £30, and went ahead. Today, among other facilities, they have two full-size snooker tables. Dads can teach sons to play. It satisfies a need. Teenage boys can go up there, play darts and snooker, and try their first ½-pints at their leisure. I am in favour of the club: it gives the young somewhere to go. We get little vandalism in our village, and today of course the girls can go too. I often wonder what my Dad would say to the girls playing the snooker tables; the children eating their bags of chips in the back room. Time marches on, as they say!

My mother's little shop was also a place where the young could meet in the long summer evenings. They would play clock-golf in the large orchard, and down at the bottom end we had a table-tennis table. They would play for the odd cigarette or chocolate bar.

Bottings' Shop, Bucks Green, 1938

My mother was strict on good manners. If the children pushed or were rude, she wouldn't serve them for a week. "You go down to Miss Hurst!" she would say, and always remembered which child it was.

One day a lady drew up in her car. Her dog jumped out and up at my mother in her white overall. Mother slapped its head. The lady was most indignant. "Well," said Mother, "I don't let my dog jump up. Why should I let yours?"

Another true little tale. It was getting dark one evening and Mother was just closing the shop when a young man came up on a motorbike. Mother went outside to serve him and he gave her what he presumably thought was a bad sixpence. But we sent it to the bank and it was half a guinea! A lot of money for ten 'Player's'.

*　　*　　*　　*　　*

Rudgwick   Then there was the Rudgwick Silver Band,
Silver Band   one of my most vivid memories when I look
                    back. How lucky we were to have such a band,
resplendent in their chocolate-brown uniform with the gold braid!

Rudgwick Silver Band
with Mr. & Mrs. G. C. Barker, Gaskyn's, 1925

*Charlie Bull, Stanford, Cooner, Len Reed, H. Francis, Higgins, P. Luff,
G. Skinner, H. Gill, R. Francis, H. Joyce, B. Reed, C. Tate, B. Tate, Harford,
H. Tickner, H. Boxall, K. H. W. Guvrell, B. Napper, Mr. & Mrs. Barker,
H. Tate (Head), B. Henley, B. White, A. Warren, F. Francis, F. Gill, S. Smith*

As we would walk up to the 'Band of Hope' or Girls' Friendly
Society of an evening, we would hear them at practice in the green
tin hut at the side of Mr. Tate's garden in Rudgwick Street. The
band had a way of holding everything together. I remember the
happy times. It really involved all the Tate family, who were a
very musical family. I can remember at one time there were nine
Tates in the village choir! This included Charlie Tate, a very big,

tall, handsome man. He did even better than all the rest: he went up to St. Paul's as a chorister! We were all proud of him in the village, as he sung at our local fêtes and concerts.

Mr. Harold Tate, the local builder, was the bandmaster. Most of the men in the band worked for him, so there was no trouble getting time off to practise or play.

The band held whist drives and dances at the hall at the side of the Queen's Head: 2/6, with £1 for top of the room in the whist. Once I won it at 12 years old. I thought I was a millionairess! Never had I had so much money. The band would play for the dances (no 'pop' groups in those days!). They were very good and 'with it'.

Then there was November 5th, Guy Fawkes' Night. We children looked ahead for weeks for the start of the bonfire. They often started building it when we went back to school after the long summer holiday. It was always at the bottom of Church Hill, in the field opposite Mr. Butcher, the butcher's. For weeks and weeks everyone collected rubbish. The Guy would be made weeks ahead and put on view in the village. The bandsmen would make the torches — pieces of rag wrapped around sticks, wired on and soaked in paraffin. All would help us children to bring the rag up to the bandsmen.

Guy Fawkes' Night

The great day came at last. Sometimes it was cold, yes, but I never remember it raining. The band would start from the Fox. The people and the children would dress up in fancy-dress. George Knight, the local chimney-sweep, would have his little hand-cart with all the torches in it — trying to guard it well from the odd firework thrown for fun!

After a quick drink at the Fox, the band would lead the way, torches held by responsible grown-ups. People watching from their garden gates had the collecting-boxes rattled under their noses. Dogs were safely shut indoors. The procession would wind its way around Watts Corner into Gaskyn's Drive, where Mr. Barker and family would be standing on the front door-steps waiting for us. He was like the Lord of the Manor and played the part to the full. When the collecting-boxes came around there was a "Thank you,

Sir!'" and a pulling of the cap and forelock. It was a case of 'I know my place and I keep it.' If the Lord of the Manor was charitable to the poor, affable to the tradesmen and generous to local improvements, the village would ask no more.

After another short tune from the band, we would all make our way to the Martlet Hotel at the station, where once more all would go in for a drink (if old enough). This was before the long pull up to the King's Head, next to the church, where for a good half-hour there would be the playing of lively tunes from the band. It really was a general booze-up, because they went from pub to pub. But the collecting-boxes were rattled around to the many people gathered along the route.

Meanwhile we children would be waiting down at the bottom of the hill around the magnificent bonfire—for hadn't Mr. Butcher the butcher saved all his pigs' bladders for the past months and blown them up? And there they were tied on and dotted all over the tall bonfire, with the Guy sitting in the old chair on the top. How could we wait? Men were in charge to see that no one lit the bonfire before the band came down the hill again. We ran around, some letting off the odd firework. Did we have a good time! Then we saw the torches threading their way down the hill with the band behind, and the people, many quite merry with the ale, were greeted with a very loud cheer.

A ladder would be placed on the bonfire and this jolly, red-faced, plump man, quite merry with drink, would climb up to the top next to the Guy to recite the bonfire prayers—about six verses in all. I remember one. I don't think we children heard the rest. We were too impatient to get the fire going.

> *Guy Fawkes, Guy Fawkes,*
> *It was his intent*
> *To blow up the King*
> *And the Parliament.*
>
> *I see no reason*
> *Why gunpowder treason*
> *Should ever be forgot.*

It would go on and on, with shouts of "Come on, Billy!" Then there would be a yell as some over-enthusiastic person would throw his torch onto the enormous bonfire. This always happened and the ladder would be moved and Billy would slide and scramble down amid cheers and clapping. As the burning torches were flung on from all sides, Billy would rush around shouting "Stack her up, folks! Pile the faggots on! Let's have a good fire!" In his happy state he didn't notice it was his faggots they were burning. (In those days the nickname for Rudgwick Street was 'Faggot Street' and every house had a pile outside. Billy, by the way, was Mr. Butcher, the village butcher, my mother's friend with the rabbits.)

After it was all over, we children would make our way home back up the street. There was still life in the bonfire. We didn't want to leave a happy evening. We were happy yet scared to have seen the flames licking around the old Guy. We kind of felt sorry for him in the end. My brothers would say: "Not long to next year", as we looked for the shells of the spent fireworks in the grass verges. We were tired out. It had been a long happy evening.

This bonfire is no longer held in Rudgwick. It is sad how the beginning of the last War seemed to end so many simple, happy times.

Mr. Tate died in 1940. No more would we hear the Rudgwick Silver Band! At almost every celebration and fund-raising event the band had been there. But about that a little later.

The Flower Show was another big day the whole village looked forward to. Ladies and children would be knitting and sewing for weeks ahead. The large tent—first sign of the great day— would be put up in the field at the side of Goblin's

The Flower Show

Pool. We children would rush down after school to look around, crawling underneath the side-flaps if we could. I remember now that smell of the damp grass drying out, kind of 'musty'. Then with about two days to go the fair would come. We children would haunt the place as we watched. The men used to say: "You go get us some rags and we'll give you a free ride!" They needed the rags to polish the brass on the roundabout. Oh, those grand, galloping, brightly-painted horses! Once a year we would see them.

The organ ground out all the popular tunes in the evening in competition with the Rudgwick band, which was playing for folks who liked to dance on the cricket field. There would be swing boats. How we shrieked with excitement and cheered each other to go higher and higher! There would be booths and stalls and coconut-shies and shooting galleries. All the fun of the fair! We used to worry our mothers to give us clean bits of rag. Of course, all the fair-men did was let us ride when they tested the equipment just before the fair opened and they let in the crowds.

The fair would open about three. But at 2 p.m. we children would be waiting to see if we had won anything in the Flower Show tent, for we had collected many kinds of grasses. Every year we tried to think of something different to put the little bunches on. Sometimes we used tennis racquets. At others, pieces of cardboard. There was no cellotape in those days: we used to do it with string. Then there were the wild flowers in large stone jars. We would run all over the fields collecting them the day before. We would bring them back and place them in the copper-house in buckets till we arranged them on the back court in these jars on the morning of the great day. They had to be in the tent before ten o'clock. The prizes were 5/-, 3/-, 2/- and 1/-. We needed that money to spend on the fair. Unfortunately we never won first prize, although sometimes we got the lower ones. You see, there was this large family who lived across the common in a very old stone house called 'Gravel Pitts'. Somehow, every Flower Show, their flowers were bigger and better than ours. Their name was Cheesemore: their dad worked on the farm for very little, so their need was greater than ours. My Mother would say: "Anyone can win. Takes a good man to lose." But sometimes we would sneak up to win the Grasses Prize if what we had put them on caught the judge's eye.

There were different age-groups. To get something was all that seemed to matter. However, we were quite happy on the evening of the fair. We had no money left. My sister, Molly, was a tall, fair, slim girl and pretty. She was very popular with the young men. So we would hang around her. Maybe we would get the odd sixpence off her. Then she would get fed up with us and send us off home, perhaps with a coconut or two if the young men had shown off their skill to impress our pretty sister. We hoped they had! Before we left we would wander over to the cricket field to watch the dancing. The bandsmen were so smart, sitting under the canopy of the cricket pavilion playing their shining instruments for the happy young dancers.

When the cherries were ripe the Fox Inn would hold a Cherry Fair. On nice warm evenings it was such fun! The band would be there, playing for the dancing on the front lawn. There would be bowling-for-the-pig, *Cherry Fair and Cider-Making* the swing-boats, the little hand-turned ride for the small children, coconut-shies—and the long, long tables loaded with those lovely ripe cherries!

Whole families would come. Dad would have his glass of beer, Mother her cider, and they'd be out under the apple trees, the children running about with their bags of cherries. The band made it all worthwhile, whether you were dancing or just listening. There was no charge to go in. Mr. Stevens was quite happy to sell his beer and the people made their own fun.

The next village, out at Rowhook, would hold a Strawberry Fair. Later on the Fox would make their own cider. I can hear now the thump-thump of the cider presses. We used to laugh, thinking that everything went into it, like dead rats and rotten apples! People would bring their own apples to have their cider made every autumn. We children would watch, hanging over the garden fence. We were never allowed near the presses. "We'll put you in as well!" the men would tease. This cider-making would go on for two or three days. You got used to the thump-thump-thump in time—but poor Mother didn't if she had one of her sick headaches!

Another thing that could bring pleasure and excitement to the village was the Aldershot Tattoo. [*Note:* This was later than most of the other events described in this book, so we *Aldershot Tattoo* children were quite a bit older.] Once a year for one week we would watch the old charabancs (open-tops) go by, the traffic building up in the afternoons. The last day, Saturday, was the best: they seemed to make a day of it. With the crates of drink on the tail-board at the back, they would wave and shout. Some would yell: "See you on the way back!" My mother and father would open all day and night that week.

It was a very 'Heath-Robinson' affair. Dad would put big table-tops on trestle-tops on the hedges, and all the thick white cups were put there too. We would employ George Knight, the local chimney-sweep, to come down and stoke the big fire by the court outside the back door. We needed lots of boiling water.

Mabel Standing came down to wash-up in the copper-house. They used to come back from the tattoo about two o'clock in the morning. If my sisters were away working, they always got time off to come back and help. They never got payment or expected it. They just went back to help Mum and Dad. The opportunity was there to make money.

Father would get so excited, yelling: "Tea up!" and George would dash up with these large urns of tea. How we never got scalded was quite surprising! Dad would slop it into the cups—at 3d a cup (it was night-time, you see—more expensive). The romantic part was—and I was just the age—we used to hang all the orchard with Chinese lanterns with candles in them. For weeks we had been painting jam-jars red and green to show the way, with the white candles in them. It was my job to take out the orders of tea and coffee to the people who sat at the little tables under the old apple trees, with the colourful lanterns above. How romantic for the courting couples coming back from the tattoo at three in the morning! I used to think so. I wonder if there are couples who still remember today having passed that way on a warm June night before the War . . .

Dad kept the village policeman happy (in case he wanted to move the traffic on too soon) by placing a bottle or two of beer down by the pond in a dark corner. And directly the coach-drivers pulled up, Val and Michael—my two brothers—would whip these drivers down indoors and Mother would give them a chicken salad. And—you bet—a piece of home-made apple pie. While Mick's job was to give them all ten cigs. (That was the reason they used to stop. And—as you may guess—word soon got around among the drivers.) They chatted to Mick and Val. Mum kept them hanging about, for the longer the drivers dallied, the more the passengers spent up the top on chips, chocolates and all the other goodies on sale.

What was really funny, when I look back, was the 'little house'. All ladies want to use the toilets. They would wait in line: you could hear them giggle and laugh until it was their turn. As they pulled the door open they cried: "God! I'm not going in there!" It did rather smell!

Sometimes Dad would fix up a kind of tent affair on the front lawn, with buckets. We had a little box for pennies, but never got any in it. Val used to take the ladies round to the front lawn. He did get the odd penny. (I suppose the men just wandered off into the back garden.) To town folk it must have been dreadful but, being brought up in the country ourselves, we never really took any notice of it. (Though I am sure I would not like to go back to it now.)

Tattoo nights did not last more than three or four years, because later on they managed to get away from the tattoo in their coaches earlier — something to do with parking and traffic conditions there. The army took over and worked it all out.

Dad with his ice-cream trolley outside the Queen's Head, 1934

*Armistice
Day*

Now to get back to earlier times and the subject of the band. The sad occasion with the band used to be Armistice Day. I say 'sad', but 'proud' would also be true. For what else have you got but pride when you lose a beloved one? Today we have on the Roll of Honour in our village church the names of both fathers and sons killed in the two World Wars, the fathers in the First and the sons in the Second. Who would have thought that the sons of men who had fallen in the 'War to end all wars' would also perish in a similar way—young lads who had played with us around our village bonfire in November, on those happy frosty nights so long ago? Perhaps it is as well we cannot look ahead!

Rudgwick Church, Sussex.

Rudgwick Church in 1907

On Armistice Day everyone would meet at the Fox. All the ex-servicemen, the war widows, followed by ordinary women and children. All were very patriotic: in those days medals were worn with great pride. I remember the ex-sergeant-major with his brushed-up walrus moustache and his very loud voice. We all waited with bated breath ready to obey him. The band was in the

front. The ex-sergeant-major would give the command and we
would start the long, slow march up to the church. Waiting for us
on the hill were the men come to remember their dead comrades,
the widows the good husbands they had lost. The lucky ones who
had come to thank God on their bended knees. Meanwhile we
Brownies and Guides were thinking it was nice to wear our uniform
on the special day and march behind the band. We all knew it was
a sad, solemn day as we did our best to keep up with the parade.

   During the service in church the names of the fallen would be
read out. Muffled sobs could be heard around the church as the
grieving congregation waited for 'The Last Post' to be sounded by
one of our village bandsmen. Then there would be two minutes'
silence, and in those days it was observed by all. No one moved,
inside or outside. Everyone would stop, no matter what they were
doing, as the clock reached two minutes to eleven. If a man didn't
remove his hat in the street, it would be knocked off. We waited,
listening to the birds up on the church roof and the braying of the
donkey we loved to feed in the vicarage field.

   Then came the singing of the last hymn—and after that we
children would be free to run down the stepping-stones in the
grass on the side of Church Hill and make our way home, very
proud to have taken part.

Church Hill, showing the 'stepping-stones'

After the War, one of the young men from our village, who was serving in the army, died on duty and they brought his body back for burial in Rudgwick churchyard. We children were so excited to see the gun-carriage with the Union Jack draped over the coffin. It was drawn by six black horses, with men riding three of them. Other men were walking at the side and behind in their smart uniforms, with red plumes in their hats. The silver harness of the horses jingled and their hooves clopped as the procession made its way solemnly through the village. Like most of the village people, we watched from our garden gate to show our respect. We would have dearly loved to have followed behind, for never had we seen anything like that before, but Mother said no. It is just not done, she explained: a funeral is for private grief. So we waited until we heard the salute from the guns echoing over the wooded parkland. And then one more exciting episode was over. It had of course been a sad day for the village, who had seen the young man grow up into a strong, handsome soldier. His sister was my best friend at school.

The
Blue
Ship
Down over the river at The Haven is the 15th century Blue Ship public house. I have often wondered why it was given that name. Some say that ships were made locally and floated down the river (the Arun) to the sea. Whatever the case may be, this was a favourite half-way house for my father on our walks along the river. We would stop there and Dad would go into the ale-bar and we children sit outside on the wooden bench. How I wished I could go inside! I would kneel up on that hard wooden seat. I can feel now the bumps on my knees as I stretched to peer in that little window. Inside, the smoke hung heavily in the bar. Now and again a large cloud of smoke would be belched down the old chimney into the broad, deep ingle-nook fireplace, filling the room. The beams were low and black with age. They were once old ships' timbers. You could see the round holes in them where the wooden pegs went. Over the fireplace on a narrow shelf were the old bottles of yesteryear and the wooden racks for the old clay pipes.

Dad would be standing at the bar, drinking and talking to the man next to him, very probably a tall, square man with a fine head of hair and damp curls drying on his forehead. This man was dressed in a coarse suit with large 'poacher' pockets. (If you watched closely you would notice movement in these pockets, for in each one would be a ferret wriggling to get out.) He was a happy, red-faced, jolly man, with a red handkerchief tied around his neck and a jay's feather tucked in the band of a grey hat pushed to the back of his head. He would be supping his well-earned glass of ale after a good day of shooting.

In the middle of the bar along two long well-scrubbed tables sat the men, who would have broken their guns and have them lying over their arms or stacked up in the corner. And the old men sat by the fire, where they watched and kept warm, smoking their clay pipes. Between them, on the uneven red-brick floor, were laid out the hares, pheasants, partridges—and of course the many rabbits—they had all had that day! But the dozen or so gun-dogs and the little terriers would be sleeping at their masters' feet, though some might have an ear cocked, or one eye open, waiting for the whistle to go again.

[One little note I must add here is about a visit I made with my husband to California recently, to see our married daughter. We were taken to see Stanford University and were enjoying the very large, beautiful library. And, like many English people abroad, I went to see if there was anything British there. I took down the first large book I saw, and at the very page I opened was a picture of men drinking, with their game and dogs at their feet. Underneath it said: 'A good day's sport at a little inn in Rudgwick, Sussex — The Blue Ship'. I felt like shouting to the many people there: "Hi, everyone! I live in this village!" You feel so proud it makes you choke.]

The men chatted and told their tales—like this one they used to tell about a certain Jim Harris. Jim always came with the rabbit shoot, but he was a bad shot and longed to shoot one he could call his own. Then one day he saw a rabbit apparently just sitting in the hedge. "Jim! Jim! There be yours!" they called, and Jim let blast. And when he went to pick it up there was a label around its neck, saying, "Jim Harris's"!

Tales were also told about smugglers coming up the river. The beginning of Rudgwick Street, the corner, is called Watt's Corner, but before my time it used to be called 'Watch Corner', as the authorities did just that: they waited there to catch the smugglers with their forbidden loot.

This next little tale is one I have heard before—the place might have been Surrey, Hampshire or Norfolk, but, yes! ... it could well have been Rudgwick. I think it is too good to be left out.

Two cockneys had come down to stay for a few days in the country near Rudgwick, on the borders of Sussex and Surrey. One morning they were walking over the fields when they met an old man ("A droll old chap"), who happened to have a large pumpkin under his arm. The Londoners noticed that the old man was carrying something, although they could not quite make out what it was. Confident in themselves as town-dwellers, they thought they would have a joke at the old countryman's expense, so they opened fire:

"Good morning, Master!"

"Good morning, Zur."

"What is it that you are carrying under your arm, friend?"

"'Tis a mare's egg, Zur."

"Dear me," said the men from the city, not liking to admit to their ignorance, "It's the finest we ever saw."

"Zur," said the old man, "there's lots of common uns but this one be a thoroughbred un; that's why un look so fine."

"Will you sell it?" asked the cockneys.

"Well," said the old man, "I don't mind partin' wi' un, tho' I don't s'pose you'll give me the money I want for a thoroughbred mare's egg."

After some bargaining, the men put their hands into their pockets and paid what was asked. The old man then handed over the pumpkin, and as he did so he looked at them seriously and said, "Now mind, Zur, and do take great care wi' un, for she'll hatch soon."

Away went the Londoners with their 'mare's egg', but as they were crossing the hill just by Baynards Station the one who was carrying the prize stumbled and dropped it into one of the gorse bushes which were dotted over the field. This startled out a hare which had been resting there. In their excitement the men must have thought that the fall had suddenly hastened the hatching, for they shouted wildly, waving their hands to the group of men who were enjoying their midday break under the oak tree at the bottom of the hill: "Hi! Stop our colt, stop our colt!"

At the back of the Blue Ship runs Oakhurst Lane, the way to Billingshurst. In this lane stands Oakhurst House, where to this day you may see the twelve Botting javelin poles, with the names of the twelve Bottings that carried them. You will also see a shield and mace. *The Bottings' Javelin Poles*

The Bottings, as is well known, were a widespread family of Sussex yeomen. All the Javelin Men of the Sheriff were Bottings. In 1789 at Brighton (or Brighthelmstone), the Sheriff was supported by his twelve Javelin Men at the celebration of the Prince Regent's birthday. They wore super-fine blue coats, buff waistcoats and buckskin breeches. Their swords were sustained by blue belts over the shoulder and crested plates. Their horses had blue and buff girths and breastplates and the head-dresses were in matching colours. My father would take us children along to gaze up in wonder at the javelin poles let into the ceiling of the great hall. It is said that the party stopped at Oakhurst for a meal and the Prince ordered that the javelin poles should remain there for whoever wished to see them. No less than twelve Botting brothers were involved. My father was very proud of them—and with every right, for they were his ancestors!

But, sad to relate, we discover blemish in this race in James Botting, who seems to have possessed more nerve than feeling, having been appointed Hangman at Horsham in the 18th century. An interesting tale is told in which certain ruffians standing near the Old White Lion (in Brighthelmstone) taunted James Botting unmercifully as he was passing by, about a certain man he had recently hanged. Botting replied that he never quarrelled with his customers. One of his assailants, strange to relate, was afterwards hanged by him in Horsham on April 12th, 1817, for stealing a sheep, and another was transported for life.

Then a certain Margaret Botting seems to have come to a very low ebb, as the authorities had to buy her a spinning wheel with which she might earn her living; and then, at her death, they had to buy a shirt (or shift) to bury her in.

On the better side: through the instrumentality of Charles Botting a magnificent hoard of Saxon coins, which had been found at his farm at Chancton, was sent to the British Museum in 1866.

In Edward I's reign the Archers of Sussex were so celebrated for their skill with the long-bow that the King personally ordered one hundred to be selected from this county and sent into North Wales to preserve order. (A colony of Bottings is still to be found in North Wales and may originally have formed a portion of these warriors.) The Sheriff had to select them and strengthen the assertion.

In Rudgwick churchyard many of the old stones have been taken down and laid as a path. You will see a number with the name, Botting, on them as you walk along. But of course as people walk on them the names will—sadly—wear out in time, but not in my time.

For the "CHICHESTER 900" Festivities in 1975, villagers were asked to take part. Mrs. Anne Burge and other organisers arranged a three-minute mummers' play, representing an historic Rudgwick scene. They decided to relive again the day the twelve Botting brothers acted as the King's bodyguards. They were "the Javelin Men of the Sheriff of Sussex". A poem was written for the play. As our local yearly fête was held near the day, the procession walked through Rudgwick again, acting the scene in their colourful costumes. It was enjoyed by all. One of the marchers was Mr. Val Botting, direct descendant of one of the original bodyguards, now in his fifties and still living in the village of Rudgwick. This is the poem that was written for the play:—

HEAR YE OUR TALE FROM RUDGWICK VILLAGE

In the famous county of Sussex
Lies the village of Rudgwick fair
And our story is of the Botting family,
Who were millers and farmed the country there.

There dwelt in the village the noble High Sheriff
A man of great renown
Who protected both the peasantry
The yeomanry and the Crown.

One day in good King Edward VI's reign
The young boy King that was,
A Royal message came to Rudgwick
That through the streets the King would pass.

The King and his retinue
Would, on a certain day,
Ride through the lanes to Midhurst
With Rudgwick's men to lead the way.

The Sheriff called for a bodyguard
Of stout-hearted men and true.
Good, brave, strong men, good trusty men
To protect their King and his nobles too.

Up stood the Botting brothers
Twelve in all, we're told,
Strong as oxen, brave as lions,
Good fighting men and bold.

The brothers came from Wanford Mill,
From mills of Albury and Brewhurst.
The first to come dwelt at Gibbon's Mill;
The last to come had travelled furthest.

One brother came from Howick Farm,
Another one from Oakhurst;
Twelve Botting brothers to form the Bodyguard,
With javelins Royally purchased.

Their yeoman's clothes were laid aside,
And dressed they were in scarlet.
Their women glowed with pride to see
Their men in such great company.

Gathered before the High Sheriff,
Bedecked in their cloth of crimson,

The brothers stood all dressed and armed
With their arrows and their javelins.

The villagers assembled in a motley crowd
To greet their young King.
Dancers, jesters, tumblers came
To entertain and sing.

The procession left the Village Green
And, as King Edward greeted the passers-by,
People cheered at the joyful scene.
"Long live the King!" you heard them cry.

This was one of Rudgwick's most famous days,
The villagers waved and clapped their hands,
They sang and caroused till eventime
And danced with gay garlands.

In grateful memory of their service
For the safe escort to Midhurst,
The javelins were presented to the Botting family
And to this day can be seen at Oakhurst.

Clare Massey

In Bucks Green we have another inn, the Queen's Head. It was an old coaching-stop, with the blacksmith's forge across the road. Oh, the happy winter days when we would stand and watch the blacksmith by his bright, warm fire, under the old beams hung with horse-shoes! Sometimes Mr. Bulbeck, the smithy, would let my brother work the bellows by pumping up and down the wooden handle stretching out from the side. I loved to watch the anvils, the men beating the horse-shoes among the sparks, dust, dirt and heaps of old used horse-shoes and battered old iron. The men would sit, watch, wait and talk, while the smithy shod the horses.

Blacksmith in
Bucks Green

Next to the forge was the old toll-house where Barbara and I dropped the pike off the bender. The last turnpike was there. I once saw an old ledger which said: 'To use the turnpike at Bucks Green—1887, 4 pence.'

When my Dad went to the War, our old spaniel dog would trot down to the Queen's Head at opening time and sit outside on the grass over the dinner-time until they closed. Then he would trot home again. He did this for the whole of the War.

Then there was another old character you never saw without his bike. He said when he was drunk he could 'walk better' with his bike. Also, if he was late for opening time, he could make that last dash quicker on his bike. In a bag on the handle-bars he carried his little rough-haired brown dog, who went everywhere with his master. They were devoted to each other. One day the man was found lying in a field ill, with his old bicycle beside him and the little brown dog standing guard. It took quite a while to coax that faithful little friend away from his beloved master. Country folk say: "A dog looks up to you. The cat looks down on you. Only the pig regards you as an equal."

The Upper Smithy, Rudgwick

After the Great War, the peace celebrations (1919) were held in the cricket field at the back of the Queen's Head. Long wooden builders' planks laid on the ground were used to sit on. The organisers brought the children down from Ellens Green in open farm wagons, picking up others on the way. The children enjoyed the ride down through the village, sitting behind those great

working horses with the harness jingling. Only one thing marred
the day: on the way back there was a cloud-burst and everyone
got soaked. But we had a super time, with races to be run, prizes
to win. And what a lovely tea! First time we tasted chocolate
biscuits, I remember! And there was a firework display in the
evening, to the joy of all the children and mums and dads alike.

*Ghosts of
Rudgwick*

Everyone likes—and many people know—a
ghost story or two. Some say the King's Head in
Rudgwick has a ghost. Its presence, although not
seen, is felt in the lifting of a latch, the flicking
of a duster around the rooms. I did not hear this story until I was
well into my sixties, which makes me wonder, was it perhaps the
new landlord thinking, "We need a ghost here"?

The ghost we all knew was the so-called 'Lady in Grey' at
Baynards Manor. Many years ago, a widow, Mrs. Finchley, lived
there on her own, and had one or two ladies who came daily from
the village to help her. Mrs. Finchley said that every night, at nine
o'clock, the outside garden gate would open, with the sound of
the iron latch. Footsteps would sound on the paved stone garden
path up to the front door, which would open and close. The chair
in the hall would scrape as it moved for five minutes or so. It
would then be quiet. After a while, the footsteps could again be
heard coming up to the front door, which would be opened and
closed a second time. Mrs. Finchley would wait for the light steps
on the garden path, the garden gate to open with the rusty squeak.
It was a friendly ghost, quite harmless. All she did was to come in
every night and rest a while. Some nights Mrs. Finchley would put
the chair facing the other way, but after the ghost had gone the
chair would be turned back, once more facing up the stairs.

One day, two of the village cleaners were going up the wide,
open staircase when they saw this grey form in a dark cloak with
the hood up, sitting in the large old oak chair at the top. A kind
of light shone from it. The Lady in Grey floated or glided into the
large bedroom as the two cleaners reached the top step. They were
not frightened: it was rather peaceful. (I think it's nice. No one
minds a ghost: you feel it can do you no harm.) And these cleaners
were quite happy to enter that bedroom to clean it.

Some time later, one of the village ladies promised to keep a housekeeper company for the night in a large house further down the lane. As she started to walk up the long drive-way at dusk, she saw this misty form in grey coming down the drive towards her. (This is how she told me the tale in her 85th year.) She too said that she didn't mind, as she knew it would do her no harm. And our Lady in Grey passed out of sight behind the large flowering bushes just there. Myself, I think the Lady in Grey was company for Mrs. Finchley at the old manor house. The story goes that the Lady in Grey was once working at the large Baynards House in the park as a servant girl. Her lover was the gamekeeper, who would visit her in her rooms after dark. Well, he was caught and beheaded on the balcony which runs around the house, and the unhappy little maid caught his head in her apron as she stood below. And every night she comes to look out for him. Now this is how it was told to me. Everyone loves a love story, so there's no harm done, be the story true or not. At any rate, we leave it there.

But I will now tell my tale of Baynards House as told in the history books about Sir Thomas More, who was beheaded by Henry VIII. It is said that when his head was taken down from Tower Bridge, his daughter brought it to Baynards House, where it was placed in an old oak chest and kept there for many years. So we can see how tales are carried on, sometimes gaining a little on the way. But it is a true saying: 'There is no smoke without fire.'

Little happened in the village—as I have shown—in the way of excitement. Mostly, we made our own amusements. But Voting Day—that was enjoyed by most. The polling station was our school, which *Voting Day* meant we had a day off. That was to start with. About this time village folk used to say: "We'll get plenty of lifts with the 'car people' just before Voting Day, as we walk around the village about our work." (meaning they expected the richer people to try and curry favour with them to get their votes.)

My father was a very strong Labour man. But he wasn't— our mother used to tell us—before the Great War. He was very disillusioned in that war because the government had promised so much. When the men came back, there would be land and work

for all, they said. However, the men never got it. On Election Day
he used to make and wear red-and-white rosettes. All of us children
and even the dogs had to wear them! He would write across the
road: VOTE LABOUR, as all made their way to the school to
vote. Dad would be the first one up there to cast his vote as they
opened. Mother would get no peace unless she went too. "That's
it," Dad would tell us, "two up for Labour! At this stage we are
winning!" He so enjoyed it. As the day came near, he tried to
convert all. When people came for petrol at a garage he then had,
he would try and try. No wonder that finally they gave the garage
a miss and he went out of business! Just as well for us children
that Mother could keep on the little tea and sweet shop.

Every year there used to be a party at the Queen's Head given
by the Conservatives for all the children whose parents voted
Conservative. Well, what chance did the Botting children have?
Everyone knew my father was Labour. And just for good measure
he shouted the odds to everyone saying that he was. There was
another family, great friends of my father, and I can remember as
a child standing opposite the Queen's Head along the brick wall by
Bucks Green Place, saying to these other children, "I wish my Dad
voted Conservative. Then we could go to the party too." This is
absolutely true! It has kind of stuck in my mind all these years.

The Queen's Head, Bucks Green

And now I can take no active part in politics. I vote. I think everyone should vote. But it made such an impression on me as a child that they should separate the children because of the party the parents voted for. This made me lose all interest in politics. As the miller said, "I got rats and I keep cats. And one day I looks into a place under my mill and there I sees cats and rats feeding together out of the same trough at my expense."

Whether the workmen on the estates of the big houses voted Conservative or not I don't know. They were never quite sure. Their boss of course couldn't tell what they did. But I am pretty certain they did vote Conservative just as the boss told them on the day. As one old farm-hand said to my Dad, "Well, I've voted for the Tories ever so long, but this time I thought I'd give these Conservatives a turn!"

Never once did my father's party win in this area. But how Dad enjoyed the fight! He had such fun out of it, and always kept hoping until the votes were counted at our school. "You never know!" he used to say.

The Coming of the Trains

We once had a hotel in Rudgwick. The Martlet stood at the top of Station Road. I remember when there were white gates across. They would open and close morning and night. When the railway was built in 1865, what a godsend that must have been! The only way to get to Horsham up until then was to walk. The carrier with his horse and cart would bring parcels out from Horsham. His sign read:—
WILL DO YOUR SHOPPING WEDNESDAY AND SATURDAY AND TAKE PASSENGERS ON SATURDAY. We had to wait until 1925 for a bus service.

The Martlet Hotel

We children loved the trains as they meant to us the good times. Sometimes they meant picking up parcels from the station from our better-off relations who lived in Croydon. They had girls our age and would send their cast-off clothes. Can you imagine the excitement, especially for me, the youngest of the three, who had everything handed down? But I can still remember those high boots with the pointed toes and the black buttons. How I hated them! I soon kicked them out!

Then the trains took us on that once-a-year trip to the sea for the Sunday School outing — this was one of the highlights of our childhood. We would stand on the wire fence down the Red Footpath leading down to the long tunnel that went to Baynards Station. We would watch and wave to all in the train. The boys used to walk through the tunnel—they said there were little places in the wall to stand in if a train came. We girls were not so brave. A man who lived at Rudgwick used to walk through the tunnel to work at Baynards. He said that in the winter he would have to break the ice made from the water that dripped through the roof from a well on the top. So he kept a crowbar just inside the tunnel just for this. Yes, trains meant happy times! People would tell the time by them. I remember Mother saying that Humphry, her first child, was born as the six o'clock milk train came into Rudgwick Station. We children would also get lifts on the milk carts loaded with milk churns and driven by farmers to the station. If they thought the train was due, it was like a chariot race.

Children used to go down to the coal yard with little hand carts for coal and coke after school. Coal was 1/1d per cwt., so you did quite well for 6d! There was also a rifle range down the station yard in the bank. Most country folk would have and be able to use a gun: clay pigeon shoots were another sport men enjoyed in the village.

Our trains were with us for a hundred years. The line was closed in 1965. Now we have the health clinic where the station was and shops where the Martlet Hotel was. But Rudgwick has gained a lovely nature walk from Slinfold to Baynards Station, along where the railway line used to be. So all was not lost. Something was gained. For this is greatly used by dog-walkers, hikers and horse riders, all of whom are safe from the busy roads.

Another memory of happy times
was when we would go blackberrying
on top of Baynards Tunnel, which was
a mile long. (When the tunnel was built,

Blackberrying on Baynards Tunnel

the bricks were made on the site from the clay that was dug out.
This was very common practice in the area with its abundance of
local clay.) Our day of blackberrying would start very early. Aunt
Jane, Edwin, her son, and us six with Mother would leave at eight
o'clock for the long walk up Lynwick Street. We had large baskets
and cups—indeed anything to hold the berries. We children would
fill the cups and then empty the contents into the baskets. On the
baby's pram would be the bottles of home-made lemonade for us,
cold tea for Mother and Aunt Jane, as well as the food. Up through
Woodsomes we walked until we were level with the tunnel. This
we made our base. We would leave the food, pram and baby. I can
see now the patch of green grass under the oak tree. It was like a
little green house, cobwebs glistening in the morning dew in the
bushes. The wire railing along the side kept people off the line and
made a lovely stand from where we could watch the trains enter
and leave the tunnel. There were six a day: as we heard them leave
Baynards or Rudgwick Station, we would rush back to our base.
Mother, Aunt Jane and Molly would go off picking, pulling the
brambles towards them with the handles of their walking-sticks.
They got pounds and pounds.

We younger children would get tired after a while. But as
long as we looked after the baby we could wander off. After, we
had that lovely dinner at twelve o'clock. The pickers would return
to base. Mother was a good cook. We would have apple turnovers,
rabbit pies, coager cake (left-over pastry with sugar and currants
in it). How we enjoyed eating under the trees on the grassy floor!

After a rest, back would go the pickers while we children
would go up to the top of the tunnel to see the ruin of Baynards
Castle. It was really just a ring of old stones now, but it was used
for a look-out many years ago. We children played our games and
had our dreams there, until we heard the five o'clock train from
Guildford coming. Then we knew it was time to leave for home.
We had had a good day, scratched our legs, helped Aunt Jane out
of the bushes where she had sat down in an extra large one. But

oh, the happiness! All would have purple tongues where we had eaten the berries. We made our way home, very tired, laden down with baskets of blackberries. This day was a treat before going back to school after the long summer holidays. And we had tomorrow to look forward to. Mother would have one of her lovely baking days; blackberry pies, lots of blackberry jam. It would last us all the winter. We would run the fields picking the blackberries, but somehow that one day—picking all day, watching the trains go by, picking flowers, in charge of the baby while the grown-ups collected the free harvest and eating out under the trees—all that will live in my mind for ever.

One last thing about blackberrying. There is a saying which says: "On October 10th the devil will spit on the blackberries", so no more picking after that date each year!

As I read over the pages, I notice it is mostly about the warm, sunny, summer days that I have written. But we did enjoy the winter months too. We made a different kind of fun. The old house was cold, with the red-brick floors in the large scullery and kitchen. And then there were the bedrooms: oh, how the water froze in the jug of the wash-basin set, and in the glass I took up to drink every night! We children didn't seem to mind. We did have those old stone hot-water bottles, and of course there was a brother or sister to help warm the bed.

Aunt Trot

One thing we were lucky about: we had an Aunt Trot. In those days she was called a 'maiden lady'. She was going to get married but her sweetheart didn't come back from the War. Aunt Jane and Aunt Trot (Mother's sisters) lived just up Tisman's Common next to the Memorial Club. Aunt Trot was very, very, kind to us children. Every evening she would come down to us. We would watch for her from the window. She never forgot our birthdays. And wasn't she the one who gave us all our only Easter Eggs? One of these I remember so well — it had a 'pearl' necklace around it. I was so proud of this, I didn't want to take it off. The first night I wore it in bed it melted on my neck, much to my dismay!

Aunt Trot would read to us. She always cut Rupert Bear out of her paper. The little ones loved it. She would never forget to bring it down with her. We would act little plays in the kitchen for her, play snakes-and-ladders and ludo. She would wash us in the stone sink ready for bed, and she it was who gave us our first tooth-brush with that tin of paste with the castle on it. She would carry the little ones upstairs on her back, with the older ones holding the candle. And when we reached the large bed we would get in together and she would read those lovely stories. We were like the family that fate never let her have.

My father used to say there were three things a Botting could do: drink beer, use a gun and play cards. The first I didn't like, the second I didn't try. But cards I have enjoyed all my life. They are something you can play anywhere, right into old age, without too much of an effort and wherever you are needed, to 'make that table up'. I well remember sitting around the kitchen table with my brothers and sisters, the warm glow from the oil-lamp on our faces, as Mother and Father would teach us to play bridge and whist when we were children. There was always a whist drive, or mothers and dads went out to play in each other's houses.

Christmas whist drives were a village tradition for many, many years. During the weeks before Christmas a coach would leave Rudgwick to support each of the surrounding villages' drives. It was the highlight of our pre-Christmas plans. At ten years of age we would start to join in the excitement, getting ready and dressing up, of course. We were quite good players at that age, having had older brothers and sisters always at hand to show and help us. I always notice grown-ups are kind to children when they are learning, even if when I was young the men did give a grunt or two if you led the wrong card. We never said a word when Dad was teaching us. "Tell me not them!" he would growl if we got things wrong. Loxwood Christmas whist drive was unusual: all the main prizes had feathers—turkey, geese, ducks, chicken. There they were laid out and there were dozens of rabbits too. Everyone was hoping to win their Christmas dinner. If you hadn't got a prize, you would often have a coney given you. At one drive I remember a man dropping a bottle of whisky in the snow as he got on the coach. All the men fell to their knees. They were dead serious, over the loss. Whisky was a rare luxury in those days, to be had only by the Rich.

Some winters we would have snow. Then the ploughed fields looked like left-over Christmas pudding with sauce on it. We would get a piece of galvanised iron, turn the end up, put string through to guide it, and away we would go down the school hill or sometimes the field at the side. But there was a brook at the bottom, so we had to be sure to turn in time or we would land in the water. One winter I remember it was so cold we went sliding on the river down by Wanford Mill and watched the ones that had skates on showing off what they had learnt on their winter sports holidays. That was the year the birds froze on the trees. And we had to pour hot water down the pump outside to get the water up from the well.

Water from the Wells   We were lucky we had a well with a pump. I can remember the well down Wanford Lane and old Mrs. Merritt from the toll-cottage and her neighbours carrying the water up using the yoke across their shoulders. Another street well was opposite the old Plough Cottage in Rudgwick Street. Years ago that was an old ale-house. They got the water from the well to make the ale. The row of cottages there also used it. Lavender Cottage, higher up Rudgwick Street, had a well in the sitting-room.

The King's Head   Before we leave this part of Rudgwick. I must tell you a little about the King's Head, right up the top of the hill. Parts of this public house are actually older than the church because, as they found out afterwards, the King's Head was used for the workmen who worked on the church. They lived where the cellars are now. This of course is common sense. If you were making a structure like a church, which would naturally take a long time, you had to house the men. When they did a lot of repairs up there quite recently, they found the living-quarters underneath, with the old brick oven and built-in copper where the workmen lived with their families while working on the church.

We heard many tales about this place, like the one about the tunnel that runs from the King's Head and comes up inside the church. Perhaps it was used to keep the men dry when they went to the many meetings in the church. Or more likely it helped them not to be seen nipping back too often for the odd drink. Local people tell the tale of how they never found "that gurt ol' bell"

The King's Head

that was being taken by boat and ox-cart all the way from Rome to Rudgwick Church when it rolled off into the boggy meadow at Dedisham. The story goes that they managed to get a chain under it but it kept slipping back in. A witch from the crowd then said she would bring up the bell if no one spoke a word. If they did, she warned, the devil would get it. The cart, she said, must be pulled by a team of white oxen at midnight. Well, the oxen were found and everything was going all right. They rigged up a tripod, dropped a chain down, and were lifting the bell out and just slipping a plank under, when some ninny yelled: "In spite of all the devils in Hell—We have got the Alfoldean gurt bell!" With that, the plank snapped, the devil gave a tug and the bell fell back into the marsh. And, as far as we know, it is still there, as it hasn't been seen since.

The King's Head was a coaching-stop with accommodation for humans and horses alike. George, Prince Regent, used to stop there on his way to Brighton. One day, when he was dressed as a peasant, he was served a rotten joint of mutton. The landlord apologised, saying he would always serve good meat from now on. Just then the landlord's son called out from the doorway, "Father, was that the rotten sheep you were saving for the fair which you have just served that gentleman?"

At the bottom of Church Hill is the Village Hall, which was built to commemorate Queen Victoria's Diamond Jubilee in 1897. This little hall was well used for such things as the Girls' Friendly Society and Penny Readings once a week. Dr. Boxall took a great part in it. We would sing, recite and act little plays, and our parents would come to watch about once a month. And we had the magic-lantern shows: they were a winter treat for going to Sunday School.

*Our
Well-Loved
Doctor*

Our Dr. Boxall was well loved. He had a lame foot. I remember him coming up our stairs with his special kind of walk. Four of us were in bed with the chicken-pox. You would put all the children together in those days. Mothers thought that if one got it then they might as well all catch it. There were also doctors' bills to pay every time they called. But our doctor didn't seem to take much. He only made the ones pay who could. I remember having chicken-pox so well. Just at that time the baby chicks were running on the lawn. "You might have got it from them!" the doctor joked. He went around in a pony-and-trap until he bought the first motor car in Rudgwick. It was a lovely green colour, with lots of brass fittings— we children thought it wonderful. We rushed to the gate to see it every time we heard it coming. The doctors in those days would do most things, including the pulling of a tooth if need be.

Dr. Boxall's car

After Dr. Boxall left us a new doctor came, who seemed keen for all the children to have their tonsils out, including us six. We used to play 'mums-and-dads' and 'doctors-and nurses'. The one who was the doctor always had to walk with a limp—until the new doctor came—we quite thought all doctors did!

As I have said before, we made our own fun—but, oh, the excitement when a plane made a forced landing in a field on Howick Farm because it had run out of fuel! We ran all the way down there just to stand and watch. Then there was the joy of hearing the sheep being driven along the Loxwood Road. We would rush to our stone steps. Dad would yell: "Don't let them in!" As we sat and watched the sheep passing by, packed so tightly, the dogs would run backwards and forwards all the time. They would go miles, walking by day and moving into a field at night. We would also watch the farm-wagons coming back from Guildford market. The farm-workers would walk there and back, bringing the cattle back in the wagons with a net thrown over them. They would take all day, stopping to feed and water the horses on the way. All worked long hours for little money, but it was a slow-moving and happy time. There was no need to rush, and when they arrived home the horses had to be seen to first, bedded down and so on, before the men could have their evening meal and rest.

Before the motor cars, the carter's pride would be a wedding. The wagon would be decorated. It would take hours to make all the decorations for the horses. But it was a lovely sight as they set off for church, the bride and all her guests in a brightly-painted wagon, bedecked with flowers.

And I also remember coffins being taken to church draped in black crêpe. In the country all footpaths lead to the church.

Horses were part of our lives. If a person was very ill, there would be straw laid outside his house to muffle the sound of the horses and wagons as they passed by. When 'Woodfalls' at Tismans Common was destroyed by fire, a servant-girl told me she remembered seeing the horse-drawn fire-engine from Horsham rushing up the long drive. There used to be a joke which went: "Yes, we will put your fire out if the horse isn't on the milk round!" But I don't remember many fires; in fact, 'Woodfalls' was the only one I can remember. The maid said she was in the house alone with the boss when she pointed out the smoke coming from the roof. But he didn't do much. The house was completely gutted. Not too many questions were asked and if you were in service you 'kept your place' in those days.

Rich people used horses for pleasure. But the rich made that needed work for the poor, and the horses did make the land easier to work for the men who used it, and they were well loved.

*   *   *   *   *

**School
Days**

I could hear Mother calling as I awoke from my second sleep: "Peggy! Get up! You will be late for school!" From the noise of the chatter downstairs Peggy knew her brothers and sisters were already up and had eaten their breakfast by now. She jumped from the bed and took a quick splash in that cold water in the china basin. It didn't take long to dress. She rushed down to the warm kitchen for that plate of porridge her mother had waiting. Mother sat with her as she ate her own. The others had gone to school. Just then the sound of the first bell could be heard, Clang! Clang! Clang! Never once had Peggy been there to pull that rope with the scarlet woollen handle which was fixed to the one bell in the little tower, up in the roof of the school. Never was she waiting in school for it to begin. Mother was talking: "Why are you always late, Peggy?" "I won't be today, Mum!" she shouted back, as she dashed out of the door, up the long court, and made it into the lobby just as she heard Mr. Bacon reading the register. "Peggy Botting!" "Yes, Sir!" she called in a loud voice, as she slipped into that wooden desk with the fixed bench seat, next to her friend, Betty Skinner. The china inkwell was full and in place, slotted into the desk. (It is just as well some children got to school on time to do all those odd jobs.)

The older children had to help the younger ones with their knitting and sewing. Often, when you went over to help, they would say, "I only put up my hand because I wanted you to sit by me." The big girls had to darn the teacher's husband's socks and mend the sheets and learn how to put on a patch. In the season, if the schoolmaster got a brace of pheasants (sort of perks, as it were) from the 'gentry'—which he often did—we girls would get the odd copper for picking them after school. My two sisters did quite well at school, but they were always so busy doing the odd jobs for the teacher that they never had much time to settle down to real school work. Molly, my elder sister, wrote an essay on 'Britain's Birthright'. Mrs. Barker from Gaskyn's presented her with a book, *The Story of the Empire,* and a medal. I remember it well: it was in 1926, the same time as Eileen Tuff was congratulated on her success in the scholarship exam. (All the time I was at school it was almost unheard of for anyone to pass *that* exam. In fact I can remember no other, although I think a few did later on. My brother, Val, went to Horsham to take an exam, but he had to answer questions on Algebra, which he had never heard of.)

To be honest, I never did enjoy my school days. I did love to write essays, but I never could spell. The master would give spelling tests all around the class-room. I would glance at the clock and think, "He'll never get to me by 12 o'clock." But—just at the end of the lesson—he would point his finger at me and snap, "You spell that, Peggy." I would stand up. Too afraid of saying the wrong letter, I would whisper to my friend: "Tell me, Betty; I will give you some sweets." Sometimes she would, sometimes not—how I hated those spelling tests, as I stood there, trembling, trying to blurt out the right letters in the right places. Everyone hates to be made to look silly. All my life I have had trouble with spelling. Yes, I do have a dictionary, but what people cannot understand is that a bad speller never knows which letter comes next after you have looked up the first one, and if like mine your teacher (when you were young) was a bully, it will stop you all your life.

But we had fun as well. Some girls had long plaits, which would be dipped in the inkwell or tied to the girl sitting in the same desk if she also had plaits.

In needlework classes we would have to make felt slippers, as on wet days the children got their feet soaking wet—there were few Wellingtons in those days. Some children came in wooden clogs and would walk two miles to school from Tismans Common. We had two large iron stoves with railings around them: I can see now the steaming jackets and jerseys drying out on the rails.

On cold, frosty mornings we hung around the fires. When you came in, the first thing that struck you was the delicious smell, for on each stove was a large white enamel jug full of lovely piping-hot cocoa, for the children to have with their sandwiches at dinner time. I have asked older people about their early school days at Rudgwick School and all seem to remember the jugs of cocoa, remembering the happy times and the good things that give comfort in life.

How different the school days were in those days. The boys had to dig the schoolmaster's garden, sweep up the leaves and weed out the grass in the spring and summmer, sometimes two or three times a week. They seemed to enjoy it—better than lessons, I

Rudgwick School Gardening Class, 1933

expect they thought. I remember the playgrounds. The boys' and the girls' playgrounds were separated and the door let into the high brick wall was very high (over six feet) and always locked. We girls tried to peep through to see what the boys were up to. It was never heard of for the girls to go into that side of the school to play with the boys. We had quite a few children who belonged to the Plymouth Brethren. They never came into school until after prayers, and if there was ever a religious talk they always put their hands up and were excused. I used to think, well, there is only one God, why all the fuss?

On Empire Day, May 24th, the Union Jack would be run up and we would all stand around it. The piano would be wheeled out into the playground and we used to sing, "Land of Hope and Glory" and "There will always be an England". The girls would wear white dresses if they had them, and carry little red-and-white bunches of flowers, while the boys would wear buttonholes the girls had made. After a talk on Empire Days, prayers were said and the flag was saluted. After the singing, the school governor would say, "Half Day!" amid cheers of hip, hip, hooray! How we enjoyed that. We didn't get many half days or days off, as they were usually only given for Royal weddings and funerals, but on Empire Day we knew we would get one for sure, and in the summer time—which was a bonus.

The headmaster was a Mr. Bacon. He was a man who had very bad health, a thin weedy kind of man with a tiny little Hitleresque moustache. He was very, very strict. I remember he used to walk up and down by the desks. If you were doing anything you shouldn't, he tapped you on the knuckles with a ruler. There were a lot of big families in those days, very poor families. I remember especially the ones that lived down Barnsfold Lane, Tismans Common. Their parents worked on Pallinghurst Farm for 15/- per week.

Mr. Bacon could never really have control of the class. I think the boys realised this and played him up. Once he went to cane a boy (in those days they did cane the children) and four rough boys knocked him down on the floor. We girls did nothing—just sat in the class. I never really knew the outcome of that, but I do not think the boys were punished. However, I do remember four village boys being taken to Horsham for breaking the white cups on the telephone poles by throwing stones up at them, and for breaking drainpipes in Farley's yard. They were all given the birch. I remember seeing them come back off the bus — there was no question of parents interfering or even going with them. The boys did wrong so they took their punishment—but I do not remember damage to other people's property happening again.

As I have already told you, the children were caned in school. I remember this one mother, Mrs. Lilywhite, who was always up at the school, complaining because her children had had the cane or whatever. (It wasn't always the cane on the hand; sometimes they bent them over a desk and whacked them in those days.) Mrs. Lilywhite's children were very naughty: they were the ringleaders and they were the ones who got the headmaster on the floor when he was trying to beat them that day. Mrs. Lilywhite was an enormous woman and she was very fond of drink. She would go into the Fox Inn in those days. (In fact she is the only woman I ever remember seeing using a pub when I was a child.) She used to come up some mornings at eleven o'clock, have a drink or two, and then go along to tell the headmaster off for hitting her sons.

I think it was more or less the drink talking. Sometimes she was absolutely rolling drunk, staggering down the path on her way home. (Once she was so drunk they had to put her in a wheelbarrow and wheel her home. When the pub had closed at two o'clock, she was incapable of walking. They had to push her for two miles, as she lived down the end of The Common. But no one would have been very concerned about this: you would often see the odd character sleeping off the drink in a ditch. Once they found this old boy lying in a cart rut along Barnsfold Lane, after having too much home-made cider. His friends just picked him up and took him home in the passing farm cart. Wasn't it nice? In those days everyone knew each other and helped them on their way, often overlooking some of the things they did, at least in our village. This was so among the workers.) For my part I think it was wrong to interfere. If we were punished at school and went home and told *our* father, he would say, "I am sure you deserved it", as most parents did — they never took part. And in Mrs. Lilywhite's case, as I said, I am sure it was the drink talking.

Once or twice a week we were taken out into the playground in classes for 'drill' — a kind of 'keep fit'. We enjoyed the break from work. We sometimes had sports at the back of the Queen's Head, if we played against another school — but this was not very often. Our playing field was down the dip behind the school, by the little brook, where the girls and boys would play stoolball or rounders, maybe on a Friday afternoon. We didn't get much play time — it seemed to be all work to me.

School Dinners

We would have a school concert about once a year, mainly for the boot and shoe club. Mrs. Bacon, the headmaster's wife, organised most of these. She worked very hard for the children and it was she who started the school dinners, in the little room under the Infants' Room. The two rooms were connected by a service lift worked by hand: fifty hot dinners were served. Mrs. Holman from Hyde's had generously provided the funds to equip the kitchen. Mrs. Bacon was wonderful and worked so hard to serve those dinners. You can imagine how the children enjoyed them — I am sure in lots of cases this was their only hot meal of the day. Ten years later that little kitchen had seen the hundred-thousandth meal served, all thanks to that little lady, Mrs. Bacon, and her helpers. You must remember there was no main water laid on. That didn't come until 1936, when the school was wired for electric light. I remember the water was brought out from Horsham in a large tanker. We had earth closets, which the local builder would take care of.

The school cleaners would work very hard for little money. A lady in her eighties told me her mother cleaned the school many years ago for 1/- per week. She had to light the fire on Sundays as well, as Sunday School was held there. The faggots would have to be chopped and the coal and coke brought in. All this in addition to keeping the school clean, staining the wooden floor too. The lady said that as a child she would have to run down to Wanford House every week to get her mother's shilling from old Mr. Botting. He was a kindly man and after she had signed the book for the money he would say, "Go round to the kitchen door and they will give you a glass of milk and a piece of cake." This was a treat in those days, so she was always willing to run that errand. But, aside from this, she was in awe of that stately old gentleman with the white beard, sitting at his desk in the red leather seat: the lovely carpet on the floor, the large grandfather clock and the hunting pictures on the walls made a great impression on her, coming as she did from a little cottage with stone floors and home-made rag rugs on the floor.

We had our 'seasons' at school. They never started at any set date, but one day, for example, a hoop would be brought to school and then for the next week or so *Our 'Seasons' at School* everyone would have them: wooden ones for the girls, iron ones for the boys. We would run for miles, bowling them along—we didn't have the traffic on the country roads then, and there were no pavements in the town, so we had more space. Then suddenly hoops were out and there were the spinning tops made of wood. You set your top spinning by winding your piece of string round it and then, retaining firmly in your hand one end of the string to which it was tied, flicking it to the ground. But to keep it spinning you had to start whipping it with your string. I wasn't very good at that and it wasn't long before my top would start to wobble and fall on its side in spite of my frantic lashings.

What I really liked was the flicking of cigarette cards up against the wall. If one fell on top of yours you got yours taken away, but if you were lucky you could pile up quite a bunch, and we had such fun swopping the cards. We would get whole sets—of birds, flowers, cricketers, film stars—worth a lot of money today. Then there was skipping and hop-scotch, bouncing the ball in those numbered squares we drew on the playground or back court, or maybe we would get a flat stone which we would kick along, hopping on one leg. While we girls were up to this, the boys would have their conker time in the autumn. Boys would climb the trees after the fruit that was spiked like mines, to get the best and biggest, which were then dangled on pieces of string. They would plumb each other's until they found the winner. Some boys used to pop their conkers into mother's brick oven after baking day to make them hard. They would then take a long time to break, but it wasn't quite fair.

Like most children, we enjoyed the snow and ice and if we were in school, and it started to snow, we would keep glancing up at those little windows with the ropes to open and close them. You could almost hear the prayers, "Please God, do not let it stop before it is time to go home." But never, never, were we allowed to make a slide in the playground (and it had a nice slope, too— such a pity!) If we did try to make one, the next day we would find the ash from the fire emptied all over it.

The Floods
Perhaps on a wintry afternoon there'd be a knock on the school door and it would be the carter who worked on Howick Farm on the other side of the river. As he stood there, twisting his cap in his hands, he would say that he'd come to get the children from "Wanford", because the river was rising fast and they wouldn't be able to use the footpath over the bridge. I remember how envious all the rest of us children were. The headmaster would read out these children's names and it might be only two o'clock in the afternoon as they trooped out and got into this horse-drawn cart, which would take them back over the river because the floods were up. We used to think, "I wish I lived down the other side of the river."

We couldn't wait to get down to the floods after school. We would rush home to pull on our boots, and rush off again with a warning from Mother, "Don't be too late—be home before dark!" ringing in our ears. They always had bad floods there. One year it came up to the Queen's Head, but that never stopped the men going down for their drink if they came by horse and cart or on horseback. For it is said that 'give the horse his head, he will never put a foot wrong, passing through water.' Even if the man is blind drunk, the horse will get him home. There was, and still is, a little stone bridge: the water would be up to the top of this and we children would watch the animals—little voles, mice—that had been washed out and drowned, floating among the debris and rubbish. If we saw a little creature struggling, we would hold out a long stick and try to help it.

There were not many cars about in those days. When the drivers used to say to us, "Can we get through the floods?"—because they were right over the road—we always said, "Yes", whether they could or not, because when they got stuck we used to go in there and push them out, and they would always reward us with a sixpence. So we always told them they could get through. It couldn't have done the cars much good as they spluttered to a halt in the middle of the water. As I think of it now, they could have gone the long way around by Roman Gate. Maybe they wanted to show off a bit. It was only the moneyed people who had cars in those days, mainly 'young bloods', as they were called.

Over by the mill they kept pigs up on the high banks. When the floods came up they would pick them up in a rowing boat. Otherwise they would drown, as a pig is the one animal that cannot swim. The men would take the pigs to the mill, where there was a kind of stable doorway which they put the pigs over. The pigs found a lot to eat—chaff, odd bits of meal and wheat—and would stay there quite happily until the water went down again. Some years later, they cleaned out the river, cutting the banks and the trees so that the water could get away faster.

The fishing club that was started so long ago—in 1931—is still flourishing. I went to a preliminary meeting with my Dad at the Queen's Head as a child in 1930. Often I think you are lucky if there is a river running through your village, for the pleasure it gives. What nicer occupation on a lovely summer evening than to sit by the cool river to fish and dream?

Our Rudgwick School is still in use for the infants. A new school was built in 1972 in Tates Way, more in the middle of the village, but by the time it was ready there was not enough room to accommodate all the children. The village had grown so much over the past twenty years and the powers-that-be who had allowed all this new development had not looked ahead. So the new school was too small and the children had to be divided.

Children arriving in Victorian clothing

*Rudgwick
School
Centenary
1880-1980
(May)*

In 1980, the Rudgwick Primary School celebrated its hundredth birthday. On one day, all the teachers and pupils dressed up in Victorian clothing—every one of 186 pupils. It was a marvellous day—the school was open to all. The children had been working on displays about the life of their school over the last hundred years, and each class studied twenty-five years. Class 4 did the most recent years, Class 5 the Victorian years, Class 6 from

1936 to 1953 and Class 7 the years following the reign of Queen Victoria to the mid-1930s. The two World Wars were very large events, so these had to be class projects too.

Centenary Classroom

In the Guildford Road school, to help provide the atmosphere of a hundred years ago, one classroom had set up an old-fashioned blackboard and easel, and three old desks with inkwells in place. As I looked, it all came flooding back, and I had the great desire to slip into that desk again—it was almost overwhelming. No, I could not make it! But it was a lovely day.

Some of the pupils arrived in the morning in a horse-drawn carriage, and there was a parade down through the village to a fair. Many of the villagers dressed up, loving to take part, including the 'new' folk, for this is what village life is all about—taking part.

Our very first school in Rudgwick was in Lynwick Street, in between the Old School House and the cottage next door. It was just one long, narrow room. When they built the new school on the Horsham-Guildford Road in 1880, the room again became part of the Old House which took its name from it.

I have tried to tell you of the simple things that we children of the village enjoyed when we were young. Like the Maypole dancing once a year and how the young girls loved to dress up with flowers in their hair, skipping round the pole, winding the ribbons in and out. Like the long summer days when Mr. Hoad and his helper, 'Jack', would tar the roads through the village. I can still smell that tar and love it even today. One 'whiff', and memories come flooding back – of the tar barrel with the funnel belching thick black smoke, the bright fire underneath to heat the tar, turning the tap to fill the watering-can, pouring the tar onto the road . . . We children would crowd around, with yells from 'Jack' to "Stand back! Stand back!" Then, before the tar set, they would throw gravel on top with a shovel, from an old black wheelbarrow. Then we couldn't wait to walk on the road—and would get tar on our socks, shoes and legs, which Mother later made us clean off with a little paraffin and a piece of rag. We had to rub hard.

One day a hot-air balloon came down behind the Red House. We children went rushing up after school and two boys were given a ride. They didn't go very high and couldn't even see over the side —I remember one boy's nose started to bleed—but you can imagine the thrill. If only we had been brave enough to have a go! But in those days girls stood back and let boys lead the way.

On warm summer days we would go with Aunt Trot to pick cowslips in the field by the railway lines at Swaynes. Mother needed those sweet-smelling little flowers to make wine. We loved walking through the woods, hearing the first cuckoo, the smell of wild garlic-like onions. We knew just where to find the first primrose, the 'totter grass' to go with the horse-daisies that grew in the Fox Meadow, or the wild shepherd or dog roses on the banks. To this day you can see the carpet of bluebells up Cooks Hill, just a stone's throw from the main road. The cars rush down to the sea every weekend—what do they miss? If they would but wait awhile!

I have always wanted to write down something of the happy times I spent in my childhood—the closeness of family life, having brothers and sisters to share the laughter and tears, the home where money didn't seem to matter.

We looked forward with joy and excitement to that one day of the year when we went to the Sea. The little joys of life matter most and I hope whoever reads this book will get much enjoyment from it. To the old Rudgwick people my hope is that you can say, "Yes, I remember"; to the new folks in the village I say, "Welcome. This is what Rudgwick was like in between the Wars before you came to live among us." I still live in the village, but now our end of the Fox Inn is joined to the public house. They keep the beer in our old kitchen—wouldn't my father have enjoyed that!

Peggy, Val, Michael, Molly, Edwin (cousin) and Barbara

We all look for that 'pot of gold'. How well I remember the warm summer day when, after a quick, light shower, that glorious coloured rainbow seemed to end in the little copse at the top of Fox Meadow. How I ran through the long grass with the horse-daisies and golden buttercups — only to find when I reached the little copse that the rainbow end was further on, still just out of reach. Now I am older and looking back over these happy childhood memories, I realise that I did find my 'pot of gold' when I was quite young. For I was one of the lucky ones in life.

THE END

INDEX